Teaching and Celebrating Advent

Revised Edition

by

Patricia and Donald Griggs

Illustrations by

Mary Corman

Griggs Educational Resource

published by
Abingdon/Nashville

© Copyright, 1974, GRIGGS EDUCATIONAL SERVICE

Abingdon Edition 1980
Second Printing 1981

ISBN 0-687-41080-0

Teaching and Celebrating Advent

TABLE OF CONTENTS

Introduction

As a child, I was raised in churches where Christmas, Palm Sunday, Good Friday and Easter Sunday were the four days when special services were planned. I was not aware of the many other significant days and seasons of the church year. It was not until Don and I were in our first parish that we really became aware of the joy that could be added to our worship by experiencing the rich liturgy, traditions, and background related to the church year. The tradition of actually celebrating Advent and becoming aware of the meaning of Advent started for us about ten years ago, in our second parish.

Since then, we have tried to help others become more aware of the church year. We feel these traditions should not be lost, but should be rediscovered each year.

In the opening monologue of "Fiddler on the Roof" we hear the words:

> "How do we keep our balance? I can tell you in one word — Tradition! Because of our Traditions everyone here knows who he is, and what God expects him to do. Without our Traditions life would be as shaky as a fiddler on a roof."

I believe there is a lot of truth in those words. We would like to encourage persons to discover, create and maintain some meaningful traditions which will reinforce their belief in and love of God.

TEACHING AND CELEBRATING ADVENT is an attempt in this direction. Don and I have saved plans, program notes, resources, and experiences and have put them together in this book to share. Much of what appears in this book was originally published in a set of eight pamphlets. However, we have attempted to revise, refine, and add new materials in this book. Everything in this book has been tried and tested in the classroom and in our family. We hope the book will serve to stimulate your thinking and planning, and that you will find the book practical and useful.

Patricia Griggs
Livermore, California
1974

2

Thinking About Advent

The celebration of Advent begins four Sundays before Christmas. This is a period of preparation for the coming of Christ. Advent is a time for anticipation, action, and reflection. The word ADVENT means literally "coming."

> Christ *has come* into our world
> Christ *is coming* into our lives
> Christ *will come* in fulfillment
> of hope for a new world of peace and love.

Advent is a time for preparation. We read of the prophets' expectation of a Messiah. We think about what the connection is between the prophets' message, the recognition of Jesus as the Messiah, and our lives today. We prepare ourselves spiritually for the coming again of Christ at Christmas.

Families seem to be drawn closer together during this time of year. The excitement of selecting presents, decorating the house, planning special family get-togethers can facilitate the drawing together of the family. This same excitement can also become an obstacle to families who want to refocus their attention and readjust their priorities during this time of preparation and anticipation.

The question that confronts persons in churches and families is, *"How can we prepare ourselves for the coming of Christ in the midst of this busy season?"* We can take time for teaching in our homes and classrooms so that persons young and old will be ready to celebrate the gift of Christ to the world. We can refocus some of our attention from the distracting, commercial elements of Christmas preparation to the more personal, meaningful features. We can readjust some of our priorities for time, energy and money.

Fathers travel. Youth are involved in a myriad of activities at school and church. Mothers are busy meeting the needs of the family as well as serving in community programs. Meals may be eaten in shifts. Tensions and anxieties increase because of the pressures of buying presents, addressing and sending cards, decorating the home, cooking for additional guests, attending open house parties, school and church programs. It is not surprising that in many families the preparation for Christmas involves frustration and disappointment instead of being filled with enjoyment in the experience of sharing and celebrating the coming of Christ.

In order to have more than good intentions it takes a little courage to put some of our intentions into action. Perhaps we should ask ourselves a few questions:

"Do I have to say YES to everything I am asked to do?"

"What are some things that the whole family will enjoy doing together?"

"Are some things we have done year after year not very important?"

"What meaning of Advent do I really want to experience and share?"

"How can we celebrate the joy, hope, and love which is central to Advent?"

Preparing for the teaching and celebrating of Advent requires decisions. We really can decide to do what is most important for us. Advent is the time for anticipating the coming of Christ, of receiving Christ into our lives, and of celebrating his presence.

It is very helpful to us that Advent is a long period of four weeks. Even though the stores have begun to display and advertise Christmas early in November it is possible that we can counteract the heavy commercial emphasis by brief, daily thinking, talking, and worshipping together during the four weeks of Advent. This is one way that Christian families can make a claim for equal-time in presenting the true message of Christ's Advent.

Celebrating Advent in the Family

In the previous chapter we said that in order for Advent to have real meaning, we must make conscious decisions to do only those things which will contribute to a nurturing, meaningful experience for everyone in the family. We know that young children learn a great deal by observation of their parents. What do children see through us? Do they see:

— mobs of people as they are dragged from store to store?

— piles of packages hidden under beds, in closets, knowing that they are untouchables until Christmas morning?

— tired, upset, impatient mothers and fathers who spend hours shopping, baking, writing, cleaning house, etc.?

— Santa Claus, Rudolph and Jingle Bells?

— Stars, candles, angels, as only pretty decorations?

If the answer is "yes," then what concept of Christmas are we teaching?

Many families have developed exciting and meaningful traditions which help them to celebrate Advent and Christmas. By cutting down on the non-essentials, and concentrating on a few meaningful traditions families can change the above image and concept for their children and begin building a concept rich with love and stability instead of anxiety and overactivity.

What follows is a collection of ideas that have been shared with us by many different families of ways to enrich family celebrations.

DEVELOPING A FAMILY LITURGY

Many churches provide devotional outlines which families can use daily or weekly for a family liturgy. A sample of one family's liturgy called FOUR SUNDAYS IN ADVENT begins on page 29. For some families a daily liturgy may be especially important. Using a liturgy just after the evening meal is often a good time for the family to gather for 15 minutes or so. For some families the 15 minutes before the children's bedtime may be best. The important thing is for the family to agree on a time to set aside for this purpose and then stick to it.

READING BOOKS

Set aside a shelf or table top for books to read during Advent. Books could be borrowed from the library or purchased at a book store. A few books appropriate for Advent and Christmas are listed in the Bibliography at the back of this book.

A SPECIAL TRIP OR EVENT

Some families enjoy going to the city without any need for shopping but just to enjoy the window decorations, the crowds, the festive spirit. This could be combined with a trip to a planetarium, museum, park, art gallery, or other place where there might be special Christmas programs or attractions.

DISCOVERING AND CREATING SYMBOLS

Advent and Christmas are rich with beautiful symbols in shape and color. Learning the origin and meaning of symbols can be interesting. It is also possible to create new symbols to use on homemade Christmas cards, tree decorations, banners and other decorations.

TIME FOR CONVERSATION

Children and youth have many questions about things pertaining to the Christian faith. Perhaps this is a good time to be open for conversation about God, Jesus, angels, Santa Claus, peace, war, etc.

NEIGHBORHOOD CAROLING PARTY

The whole family begins at the home next door by singing a few carols in front of the house and then inviting that family to join in to go to the next house. After a number of homes have been visited and families have joined, everyone could return to your home for refreshments and a time for visiting.

FAMILY WORKNIGHT

Involve everyone in baking cookies, or decorating the home, or wrapping presents. Some families have discovered great joy and satisfaction in creating their own greeting cards and making a family project out of the preparing, addressing, and mailing of the cards.

MAKING AND USING AN ADVENT CALENDAR

An Advent Calendar has "windows" to open for the days of Advent. There are many commercially produced calendars, but they tend to not include the biblical, Christian dimensions of Advent. There is a sample calendar included in the back of this book for families to make and use. Or, you may want to design your own.

USING A CRECHE

Many families have a Creche that they put out every year. The creche may have more meaning if one figure a night is put out, or several added on Sunday, until on Christmas morning the Christ Child is added. After Christmas the Wise Men may make their way from a kitchen cupbord or a closet, to a table, over the mantle across the coffee table, etc., until they at last arrive at the Creche on Epiphany Sunday.

REACHING OUT TO ANOTHER PERSON

There are many lonely, forgotten persons in our communities and churches. Advent may be a time to reach out with friendship and caring to another person. What begins in Advent can grow through the year in a new relationship. Often Convalescent Homes, Hospitals, Orphanages and like places are overwhelmed at Christmas with persons and groups who want to give gifts, sing carols and visit with lonely persons. When Christmas is over there is a big let-down because everyone has gone back to their old routines and the visits are forgotten until next year. The most important part of reaching out, is to really connect with someone specific and maintain the relationship throughout the year.

SHARING WITH OTHERS

Advent can be a time for renewing old friendships and developing new friendships by sharing with a friend or neighbor a part of your family's traditions. There are friends far away who have not been seen for a long time. Writing a family letter or recording a taped letter can be a very rewarding and renewing experience.

LEARNING SONGS, SCRIPTURE, PRAYERS

If you have younger children in your family they may appreciate your taking the time to teach them the songs, prayers and stories that are familiar to the rest of the family but new to them. Songs, Bible passages, or prayers can be learned a phrase at a time and discussed. It may take one whole Advent season for a song to be learned, but how proud the child will be when he has learned it and can participate with the rest of the family without hesitation. Some persons may remember Advent as the time when they learned the Lord's Prayer as a young child. Have the whole family participate in the learning and repeating of the phrase so that the child feels a part of the process and not set aside as the "one who does not know and has to learn."

PLAYING MUSICAL INSTRUMENTS

Children who are taking music lessons and parents who have not played their instrument for years could have fun learning to play Christmas carols together.

HAVE A NEIGHBORHOOD CHILDREN'S PARTY

Adults are usually the ones invited to open houses and parties at Christmas. Why not invite the children who live around you to your house for a short, children's party? Playing a few simple games, singing some carols, having refreshments are all that is needed. It is a good way to meet children you may not know well and an opportunity for your family to offer good will to the neighborhood.

MAKE NEW FRIENDS AT CHURCH

One Sunday the congregation quietly passed a clipboard around one side of the sanctuary during the service. On the clipboard were several sheets of self adhesive labels. Persons who wanted to be guests for dinner signed their names and addresses on the labels and the number of children in their family. Then the clipboard was passed along the pews on the other side of the church and those who wanted to be hosts took a label off the clipboard and stuck it on their coat. After church the two families found each other and made plans to have dinner together to get acquainted. A couple of weeks later the same process was repeated, only the clipboard was passed on the opposite sides of the sanctuary so that the persons who were guests last time could be hosts this time.

ANOTHER FAMILY'S EXPERIENCE OF ADVENT

The most carefully planned programs and best intentions in the world cannot always anticipate what will really happen. Seldom does a Sunday lesson, a party, or a family's attempt at establishing a family tradition come off "according to the book." Some time ago in the magazine *Presbyterian Life* there appeared an article which should give us all encouragement as we attempt, in our families, to make changes for the more meaningful celebration of Advent and Christmas. We reproduce the article here for your enjoyment.

"HOME-STYLE, ADVENT CEREMONY"*
by Sally M. Jarvis

A few years ago, our church gave us a pamphlet describing a typical home Advent ceremony. This is usually a simple ceremony in which the whole family participated. A candle is lit on a wreath on each of four Sundays before Christmas. The family may say a prayer, read a passage of Scripture, or sometimes sing a hymn. The pamphlet was full of good ideas on how to conduct this ceremony, but we couldn't help wondering what kind of family the writer had in mind. I don't think it could have been ours.

The cover picture showed a mother and father, both looking peppy, and a boy and girl, both smiling. All were looking at the Advent wreath in the center of the picture. The boy and girl were (a) neatly dressed, (b) had their hair combed, and (c) were not fighting over their turn to light the candle.

In our family instead of a brisk-looking mother and father would be two rather weary individuals, who have never really recovered from their headlong dash to get themselves and the children to the 9:30 service, not to mention the coffee hour, Sunday dinner at Grandmother's, and junior choir at 5:30.

The pamphlet children — two in number, neat and tidy — would be replaced by four — all messy. The boy would be in jeans, the girls in slacks. The baby would still be in her pretty Sunday dress, but because she'd spent the day sleeping and eating in it, it would stick to her fat tummy in comfortable wrinkles.

The pamphlet had the first child say, "I light this candle on the first Sunday in Advent."

In our house the first child said, *"It's my turn to light the candle."* The second child said, *"You did it first last year; it's my turn!"* Third child: *"Daddy, you promised me last year that I could do it first this year."*

Father: *"Look, there's only one candle . . ."*

First child: *"Yes, and it's my turn!"*

Finally Father had the inspiration of having one child strike the match, one child light the candle, and one child blow it out. He was lucky the baby was too young to speak up.

* copyright *Presbyterian Life,* used by permission.

As the little light flickered during the Bible reading, the children became still. For an instant something had been achieved.

There are other problems not covered by the pamphlet. The following year, the baby was no longer an amiable six months old, but a tyrannical and unreasonable eighteen months old. Grandmother gave us a lovely creche with wooden figures so that the children could play with them and act out the Christmas story, as the pamphlet suggested.

Instead the boy grabbed the Wise Men, the two girls took the angels, and the eighteen-month-old disappeared behind the sofa with all the animals. No amount of talk could persuade anyone to share anything; finally a cross mother removed all figures from all children and put them back in the box. The only good thing to come out of that incident was that Grandfather, a Presbyterian minister, used it in a children's sermon (Christmas must be shared).

That year the Sunday School teachers liked the Advent-wreath idea so well that each child made one in class; now we had four wreaths on the table. This did simplify the who-lights-the-first-candle problem, but made the process so involved by the time we got up to the fourth Sunday that the brother had to make a chart telling who did what when. Once again as we sat in the candlelight, the magical hush came.

Then someone noticed that the candlelight from below was casting shadows on the ceiling from the chandelier. Because the chandelier was swaying slightly, so were the shadows, and the brother decided that this looked just like Superman. *"It's a bird. It's a plane!"* went the cry, and the six-year-old was so carried away that she leaped up from the table and ran around the house turning out lights so that we could see the shadows better. We were plunged into darkness, with everyone shouting *"Superman!"*

The next year the baby was two and one-half; and when she saw the candles, they meant birthday. *"Birt Day TO you!"* she sang, *Birt Day TO you!"* This was really very nice and made it easy to talk about Jesus' birthday. On the other hand, that was also the year the two older sisters fought over whose turn it was to light the first candle and one finally shouted, *"Go on: Light the candle of love, dummy!"*

Five years have passed since our church introduced us to the Advent wreath. Last year the "baby"— five and one-half — could say some of the Christmas story; the other three did all the Bible reading. When the candles were lit, no one dashed from the table to put out the lights, no one sang, *"Birt Day TO you,"* no one shouted, *"It's a bird. It's a plane!"* — and I was a little sad. Our Advent ceremonies would never make the typical-family pamphlet yet I feel the baby Jesus would have enjoyed every one.

Celebrating Advent in the Classroom

Advent is a very happy season, an anxiety producing season, and often a period of frustration and confusion for children as well as adults. The anticipation of presents on Christmas day, extra good goodies baked for the Christmas season, family gatherings, and the spirit of the season makes for happiness. The asking for presents you are not sure you should ask for, and maybe will not get, deciding what presents to give, dealing with doubts about Santa and God, all contribute to anxiety.

When we face students in the classroom during Advent we need to be aware of these conflicting feelings and provide the understanding and stability of our faith that will help them find our Lord this season.

When teachers of younger children begin to plan their Advent lessons, they need to be aware that some students are questioning the existence of God as they are now becoming aware that there is not one "flesh and blood" Santa. Teachers of older students need to be aware of the need for building bridges of understanding and providing the background and content of our faith that will help the student deal with his questions about his faith and come to a deeper understanding of the meaning of Christmas. Even youth and adults are still plagued with questions and need the opportunity to deal with them. They also need the opportunity to find ways to make decisions to participate in those activities during this busy season that contribute to the preparation of their lives for the coming of their Lord Jesus.

CONSIDERING THE ISSUE OF GOD AND SANTA*

More than once persons have told me that they used to think God and Santa Claus were brothers, or that when they stopped believing in Santa Claus they really wondered whether or not God was real.

It is not surprising that persons would feel that way. If we look at God and Santa Claus through the eyes of a young child we can see why the connection between the two

1. The story about God Begins, "In the beginning God created the heavens and the earth . . ."

1. The story about Santa Claus begins, "T'was the night before Christmas.'.'."

From a young child's point of view, which story is more familiar? Does one have more authority than the other?

2. God lives in heaven.

2. Santa lives at the North Pole.

Is heaven any more real to a child that the North Pole? Probably less so. At least we can point to the North Pole on a map to reinforce that idea.

3 God is a wise old man with a beard and robe.

3. Santa is a jolly old man with a beard and red coat.

People dress up like Santa. No one dresses up like God, but children still project images of what God looks like.

4. We say prayers to God.

4. We write letters to Santa.

Is one form of communication more effective than the other from the perspective of the young child? Now there are books of "Children's letters to God" and "to Santa."

5. God gets his message to people by angels.

5. Santa gets his gifts to people with reindeer.

Is it any more likely that reindeer can fly than it is that winged, robed, feminine creatures can fly?

6. God knows everything, cares for everybody, and punishes the bad people.

6. "Santa knows if you've been good or bad, so be good for goodness sake."

Worrying whether God will punish or whether Santa will not leave gifts can be the same for young children, if these images of reward and punishment are reinforced.

It would appear from the above examples that there is good reason for young children to be confused between God and Santa.

*From "God Through the Eyes of a Child" by Donald Griggs. Published in *Essential Skills for Good Teaching* by the National Teacher Education Project.

We expect children to discover that Santa is a myth and to grow to a new appreciation for the Spirit of Christmas and the traditions of Santa originating with St. Nicholas and others. We do not stop Christmas when children discover the Santa myth. Rather, Santa takes on a new dimension where everyone can enjoy the fun of the tradition. Can it be similar with our growing understanding of God? Some of our early concepts of God are like myths which take on new and enriched meaning as we grow. It seems to me that we should encourage children to exchange images for God in their growing and learning. When Santa, living at the North pole, ceases to be "real" and is exchanged for the Spirit of Christmas, then God living in the sky ceases to be "real" and can be exchanged for a new understanding of God's power and presence through his Spirit.

ACTIVITIES FOR YOUNGER STUDENTS

Children in the second and third grades are ready for the book THERE IS A SANTA CLAUS. This book is listed in the Bibliography. There is also a filmstrip on St. Nicholas produced by Cathedral films, which could be helpful. These resources provide good bridges for the children to revise their concepts in their thinking about Santa Claus. It is also important to provide bridges for them to begin enlarging their images of God. The opportunity to talk with the students about their images and concepts of God, Jesus, Christmas, Church, prayer, etc., can be beneficial to the teacher and the student. Through an interviewing approach where the teacher asks probing questions, but does not attempt to "teach," the teacher can learn much about where the students are in their conceptual development. Then the teacher can be in a position to know what to teach and where to begin.

Third graders especially may be ready for a filmstrip or a book which relates some of the ways persons in other countries celebrate the Birth of Christ. They are also old enough to be aware of some of the customs in their own homes, and can share these with the class.

A fun way to expand this study is to use puppets to dramatize the various customs. Or, use a flannel board for which the children have made figures and decorations to tell the story of customs in other countries.

Have a Sunday devoted to music. Your class could learn some carols and visit a younger class to sing with them. Or, join another class to sing together and perhaps share some of the things they have made, or studied the past few weeks. Making some "props" to go along with the carols (pictures, rhythm instruments, Advent wreath, creche scene) could add to the fun of the singing. If you cannot play an instrument perhaps a high school student could play a guitar or an autoharp to accompany the students.

It is never too early to begin teaching children the importance of reaching out to others. Is there someone in your congregation that would welcome some children from your class? Perhaps there are some shut-ins or some persons who don't get out much who would enjoy a gift made by the children — some caroling — or a friendly visit. If you have a large class and not everyone can go, how about selecting several children to go with you on a Saturday or a day after school. Take a tape recorder and a polaroid camera so that you can take back to the class a report about your visit.

Is there something you can do around the church to clean it up — work in the garden, make decorations for a dinner or Christmas program — provide the cover for the church bulletin for a Sunday during Advent.

Part of the stability and reinforcement of our faith is found in traditions. The classroom of the younger child is a good place to begin building some traditions. Two ideas are the Advent Wreath and the Advent Calendar.

The Advent Calendar suggested in the back of the book is very appropriate for younger children. The reading of Scripture from the calendar along with lighting appropriate Advent candles and singing a couple of carols will enhance any lesson that is planned for each Sunday.

The tradition of the Advent Wreath is one that is meaningful whether practiced in the classroom, sanctuary or at home. In the classroom begin by spending some time with the symbolism of the wreath.

The wreath is round — reminds us of the never ending love of God

The wreath is evergreen — reminds us of the gift of life

The wreath has four candles — reminds us of the four Sundays of Advent.

The wreath may have a fifth candle reminding us of the birth of Christ.

The candles may be purple — the ~~liturgical~~ *traditional* color for ~~Advent.~~ Royalty - denoting Christ's Kingdom,

The Christ Candle may be white — reminding us of the purity of our Lord.

One way to approach the symbolism is to have on hand a number of different kinds of symbols connected with Christmas that are cut out of construction paper. These shapes can be: cane, star, circle, candle, cross, lamb, manger, bell, camel, donkey, etc. Show one symbol at a time and let the students tell you all the things that that shape reminds them of. End with the circle. Read the story "THANK GOD FOR CIRCLES." Hold up a styrofoam ring. Speak about the significance of the circle and explain that the ring is going to be the base for an Advent wreath. Speak about the symbolism of each part of the wreath. Then have the children make wreaths to take home, or make one for the room to use each Sunday of Advent.

Instructions for making wreaths are in the chapter, *Deck the Halls.*

ACTIVITIES FOR OLDER STUDENTS

Many persons celebrate the familiar days of the church year, Christmas and Easter, without ever realizing their relationship to the many other days of the liturgical calendar. Even if one is able to name many of the days of the church year he may find it difficult to identify the significant meanings or know the origins of these days and seasons. What follows is one way of introducing the church year. After spending some time with this process it is important to spend more time on developing the meaning and origin of the particular season or days which are current.

The teacher should note that many 4th, 5th, and 6th graders have difficulty with chronology. Some students at this age are still not able to conceptualize the order of seasons, months, or dates when holidays happen each year. For this reason the teacher may not want to put too much emphasis on this part of the exercise.

DAYS AND SEASONS OF THE CHURCH YEAR

STEP ONE

— Have persons work in pairs or triads.

— Give each group an envelope containing cut-up slips of paper with the following days printed on them:

NEW YEARS	WASHINGTON'S BIRTHDAY	FLAG DAY
ADVENT	MAUNDAY THURSDAY	LABOR DAY
CHRISTMAS	PASSOVER	VALENTINE'S DAY
THANKSGIVING	GOOD FRIDAY	HALLOWEEN
EPIPHANY	ASCENSION SUNDAY	SUKKOTH
LENT	WORLD-WIDE COMMUNION	SUMMER
ASH WEDNESDAY	LINCOLN'S BIRTHDAY	SPRING
PENTECOST	MEMORIAL DAY	FALL
PALM SUNDAY	FOURTH OF JULY	WINTER
VETERANS DAY	EASTER	HANUKKAH

STEP TWO

— Instruct each group to categorize the days and seasons written on the slips of paper. (Any categories will be appropriate.)

— Allow 5-10 minutes for the groups to sort and identify the words in order to put them in categories.

— After most groups are finished ask them to state the categories they have identified.

— Call attention to the many ways we classify the important days of our year.

— Summarize with a comment on the fact that all these days and seasons have meaning for our lives. They are the landmarks or focal points among which we plan or anticipate much of the importance in our living as persons, families, communities and as a nation.

— Such is true with the Church Year.

— Call attention to those who have categorized some of the words and labelled them as "religious days," "church seasons and days," "Christian holidays" or whatever other label they use.

STEP THREE

— Instruct the groups to put back in the envelope all of the days and seasons that are not included in the Church Year.

— Then put all the church seasons and days in chronological order.

— After each small group has placed them in chronological order, ask for the group as a whole to review the correct order.

— Leader can record on overhead projector, chalk board, or newsprint the correct order as reported by the group. Where there are mistakes or questions allow them to be recognized or stated but do not attempt too much clarification. Allow the clarification to happen as they work on the next step.

STEP FOUR

— Encourage each group to select a different season or day on which to do some research.

— Have the groups respond to the following questions:

1. What are some of the biblical connections to the season or day?
2. What are some of the historical or cultural origins of the season or day?
3. What are some of the contemporary values of celebrating the season or day?

— The following books could be helpful in doing the research:

THE YEAR OF THE LORD by Theodore J. Kleinhaus, Concordia Publishing House, 1967

HARPER'S BIBLE DICTIONARY by Madelaine S. and J. Lane Miller, Harper and Row, 1961.

YOUNG READERS BOOK OF CHRISTIAN SYMBOLISM by Michael Daves, Abingdon Press, Nashville, 1967.

STEP FIVE

— After doing research the groups can be encouraged to express the meaning and background of their season or day in one of several ways:

1. Creating a banner from burlap and felt using color, symbols, and words.

2. Create a montage using pictures and words from magazines, Christmas cards, calendars, etc.

3. Prepare a verbal report illustrated by symbols created on posters, overhead transparencies, write-on slides or some other medium.

4. Using several hymns either sung, recorded, or written to focus on specific meanings of the particular season or day.

STEP SIX

— When each group has completed their research and creativity allow them time to review how they are going to share the product of their work with the rest of the class.

— Have the presentation done in chronological order thus reinforcing the sequence of the church year.

DAYS AND SEASONS CROSSWORD PUZZLE

by Donald L. Griggs

An appropriate activity for students who may have finished their work early or who have come to class early, would be this crossword puzzle.

DOWN

1. The day and season celebrating the gift of God's Holy Spirit.
2. The day which commemorates Jesus' death on the cross.
4. The first day of Lent.
6. The happiest birthday of the year.
8. A day of victory, triumph and new life.

ACROSS

3. A day when we remember Jesus' last supper with his disciples.
5. From a Greek word which means "showing" or "manifestation."
7. The word means "coming;" the season includes four Sundays.
9. Forty days of fasting and preparation.
10. A day which recalls Jesus' entry into Jerusalem when he was acclaimed as a King.

FOCUS ON THE MESSIAH

When we read the Old Testament there are many places where the prophets express their confidence and expectation that God is going to act in a very special way to set the people free. These prophets were expecting a Messiah. Messiah means redeemer, deliverer, great leader. They had different ideas of what kind of Messiah God would send. But, their common expectation was that this Messiah, whoever he was, would do a tremendous job of setting things straight.

STEP ONE

Give each student a piece of paper with a scripture verse printed in the corner. Have the students look up their scripture verse, and determine what that passage is saying about Messiah. What kind of Messiah is that writer expecting? Have available other reference books for the students to use for further information.

Books that may be helpful are:

BIBLE ENCYCLOPEDIA FOR CHILDREN by Cecil Northcott, Westminster Press, 1964.

PEOPLE OF THE BIBLE by Cecil Northcott, Westminster Press, Philadelphia, 1967.

YOUNG READERS' BIBLE DICTIONARY, Abingdon Press, Nashville, 1969.

Suggested Passages of Scripture:

ISAIAH 9:2-7   ISAIAH 52:13   53.6
AMOS 9:8-15   JEREMIAH 31:31-34
ISAIAH 40:1-5   MICAH 5:2-4
                  MALACHI 3:1-5

STEP TWO

Each student could then draw a picture or symbol on his paper with chalk, paint, or felt pens that will convey the kind of Messiah his scripture passage was describing.

STEP THREE

Share the finished pictures and have each student report on the passage of scripture he read and the picture he drew.

STEP FOUR

Questions to discuss:

1. Did Jesus enter the lives of men the way the scriptures said he would?

2. If you were a Hebrew in Jesus' time would you have recognized Jesus as the Messiah that was written about in the scriptures?

3. What kind of Messiah are people looking for today?

4. What kind of problems do we have that need correcting?

5. If you were looking for someone to set things straight in the world today, what kind of person would you describe? What would be some of his characteristics?

QUESTIONS ABOUT THE CHRISTMAS STORY*

All of us are familiar with the Christmas story telling of the birth of Jesus. We tend to put all parts together to make one story. However, there are really two stories, two accounts of the birth of Jesus. The purpose of this lesson is to help the students realize there are two sources or traditions behind the Christmas story and to understand the meaning of each story.

STEP ONE

Divide the class into two groups. Have each group choose a chairman or leader to guide the group. Give each person a copy of the worksheet. Assign each group one of the stories to read. Have each group answer the questions from the perspective of "their" story. Allow the group to work for 10-15 minutes.

SAMPLE WORKSHEET

Read the passages of scripture as listed and then answer the questions in the appropriate column.

MATTHEW 1:18 - 2:12	QUESTIONS	LUKE 2:1 - 20
1.	What city was Jesus born in?	1.
2.	Where was Jesus born?	2.
3.	Where did Joseph and Mary live?	3.
4.	Why did Joseph and Mary go to Bethlehem?	4.
5.	What ruler is mentioned?	5.
6.	Is a star mentioned?	6.
7.	Are angels mentioned?	7.
8.	Who shows up in Bethlehem?	8.
9.	What do they bring?	9.
10.	What voices of authority are quoted?	10.

STEP TWO

Spend some time discussing the following questions:

What is missing from the part of the story you read?
Why do you think the two stories are so different?
What is the most important point about both stories?
What is your biggest question about Jesus' birth?

STEP THREE (if time permits)

Divide the class into several groups to do some additional research on specific aspects of the Christmas Story. Use both stories to find the necessary information. Be aware of which story is the source of that information.

*Quoted from TWENTY WAYS OF TEACHING THE BIBLE by Donald Griggs

Group one: The Geography

   1. What places (cities, countries, etc.) are mentioned in both stories?
   2. Locate these places on a map.
   3. Look up information about each place.
   4. Discuss any relevant points related to each place.

Group two: The People

   1. Name all the persons mentioned in both stories.
   2. Look up some information about each person.
   3. What are the major differences between the two stories?

Group three: Hard Words

   1. Make a list of the words that are hard to understand.
       (angel — Emmanuel — betrothed — etc.)
   2. Look up these words in the Bible Dictionary.
   3. Discuss the meaning of the words and write a one sentence definition on a chart to share with
       the class.

STEP FOUR

Have the groups share with the whole class the results of their research. Allow time for questioning and discussion to explore the implication of each report.

WE NEED GOD'S ACTION HERE!

Refer to and review study on MESSIAH.

Read scripture passage from one of the prophets. Discuss briefly what the Hebrews were looking for in a Messiah.

See the filmstrip LORD, COME! produced by John and Mary Harrell, available from them at P.O. Box 9006, Berkeley, California.

Look at the Pictures and Text and listen to the recording of *O COME, O COME, EMMANUEL* from the LORD, COME! kit.

Discuss: Where do we need a Messiah today?
          What does a Messiah need to do there?
          Is there any way we can "prepare the way" for the coming of God into these places in
          our world?

Work on a montage of WE NEED GOD'S ACTION HERE . . . use magazines, rubber cement, scissors, and large construction paper or butcher paper on which to mount the montage.

Conclude with short worship service from FOUR SUNDAYS IN ADVENT.

A SIX WEEK SERIES FOR CHILDREN AND ADULTS

Church Educators and those persons leading youth groups may be interested in the following outlines of extended workshop or session plans. These plans could be spread over a period of several weeks, depending on how much time you have each week.

This particular plan was used with a class of adults and children. Its purpose was to provide a class in which families could study and work together. Children from Kindergarten through Junior High were registered in the class with their parents. High school youth and other adults without children were also registered. This same plan could also be used with an adult group, a junior high group, or high school group.

The class is based on a one hour time schedule, but would work better if a longer period were available.

> 5 minutes for arrival
> 15-20 minutes for presentation of key concept
> 35 minutes for work period
> 5 minutes for clean up
> —
> 60 minutes total

The sequence of lessons uses many of the ideas already presented in this book. These sessions have some real value in that they provide an opportunity for families to work and study together, a rarity in this day and age!

Because of the time limit, each Sunday must be focused on a single specific concept, and each activity must be simple, quick to accomplish and something that young and old can both do and find rewarding. When planning these sessions be sure to have materials for the activities prepared ahead of time to cut down on the time needed to work on them. For example: When doing the banners you would have the burlap cut to size and felt in squares all stacked on the tables with glue and scissors, so that the family would have all materials needed right at their place. When doing picture lifts, the plastic and contact would already be pre-cut into various sizes and stacked on the table ready to use. The table would also have on it the tub of water, magazines, construction paper.

At the first meeting of the class several points were made to set the stage:

> Because the group is large and the time is short we ask each family to:

> > Be on time.
> > Raise their "help" sign when assistance is needed.
> > Each family cleans up their mess at their place.
> > Take home the activity to finish if not done.

> We are all learners no matter what age we are.
> We want to work at listening to one another.
> Children have as much right to express themselves as adults.

> We see the class as an introduction to the subject. We hope the family will take the opportunity to study it further at home. There will be instructions for each activity so that it can be done over again at home.

> The activity may be new to some of us. This means that what you do here may be experimentation. You may want to do the activity over again at home after you have experimented with the materials.

The routine for each Sunday will be:

> 9:00 everyone seated
> Explanation of mechanics of activity
> Motivation — presentation of subject matter
> Creating time
> Clean up
> Go to church

FIRST SUNDAY

The purpose of the session is to identify where Advent fits in the church year and to identify the symbols connected with Advent.

The family activity for the day is to make a burlap and felt banner which reflects the family's concept of Advent, using the colors and symbols and ideas presented.

Some things for the teacher to consider in presentation —

> Time is remembered by special events: Birthdays, Summer Vacation, Christmas.
> These are landmarks -— points of reference.
> The Christian has two calendars. A church year calendar and a civil year calendar.
> The church year calendar came about as churches created special events during the year to educate the congregation about events in Christ's life.
> Each church celebrates events of the church year according to what they think is important. Not all churches celebrate the same events in the same way.

Have each family look in the envelopes that were given when they arrived. If you have time follow the directions for THE CHURCH YEAR exercise on page 14. If not, have the family choose the slips which they feel should be part of the church year calendar. List a consensus on the overhead projector. Focus on Advent and Christmas. List suggestions of symbols for Advent and Christmas. Add your own suggestions.

Work on Banners.

SECOND SUNDAY

The purpose of the session is to identify where Christ is needed and where Christ is working in our world today.

The activity is to make picture lifts which can be hung on the tree, or made into a mobile.

Some ideas for the teacher to consider in the presentation:

> What kind of Messiah were the Hebrews looking for?

> What kind of Messiah came?

> The word Advent means *coming*, the coming of the Messiah. The Hebrews were looking for someone who would come and set the world right. They wanted an end to war, poverty, illness, unjust laws.

> This sounds familiar doesn't it? We have these same things in our world that we want set right.

> The difference between the Hebrews and us is that we know Jesus Christ. He taught us a style of life which makes us feel the responsibility of doing what we can to make things right and not waiting around for someone else to do it. By following the life style of Jesus, we should be able to make a difference in the world.

Use the photographs that are included in the LORD, COME! kit by John and Mary Harrell and the recording O COME, O COME EMMANUEL. We begin to get a feeling of the Messiah that *is here.* Look for a connection between what you see in the photos and what you hear in the recording, and what you feel is your mission as a Christian today.

Select pictures from magazines that will remind you of Christ at work in the world today. Make picture-lifts, frame, take home for tree or hang on wire for a mobile.

Instructions for the picture-life process are found in the chapter DECK THE HALLS, page 49.

THIRD SUNDAY

The purpose of the session is to explore traditions which can enhance the family's celebration of Advent. Special emphasis will be on the use of the Advent Wreath.

Some ideas to consider in the presentation:

> — How many Sundays are there before Christmas — counting this Sunday? (four)
> — Think about past Christmases and recall some of the traditions your family has that makes Christmas important and fun. Select one tradition to share with others.
> — Put yourselves in groups of three families to a group and each family share one tradition with the others.
> — Choose one of the three traditions to share with the whole group.
> — One tradition which families can have that is very meaningful is the tradition of the Advent Wreath.

Think about the Advent Wreath.

> The wreath is round to symbolize the never ending love of God.
> It is made with live greens to symbolize life.
> We use four candles — one for each Sunday in Advent.
> Sometimes we have a fifth candle that is called the Christ candle and is lit Christmas morning.
> The color of the candles is purple — the liturgical color for Advent.

Call attention to the pamphlet FOUR SUNDAYS IN ADVENT which has been given to each family as they arrive. Suggest that this pamphlet along with the Advent wreath can be used at home each Sunday or several times during the week.

Give instructions on making the Wreath. Each family was given a packet of materials when they arrived. The packet contained the FOUR SUNDAYS PAMPHLET, a small spool of wire, a styrofoam ring, and four purple candles. Two areas of the room had piles of fresh greens, a box of pinecones, ribbons. On the tables were several pairs of pruning shears, and wire cutters. Children were encouraged to make lapel pins, out of the scrap greens, for their mothers and to give to ladies as they arrived for church.

FOURTH SUNDAY

The purpose of this session is to focus on the Birth of Christ.

The activity is making wire and plastic symbols to hang on the tree.

Ideas for presentation:

1. We have identified Advent:
   in the church year
   as meaning "Coming"
   as a time of preparation
   as being for four Sundays and weeks before Christmas

2. We have seen that the Hebrew persons were looking for a Messiah to come and solve the problems of the world. That Jesus' coming did make a difference in the world. That Jesus is present in our world today through us and the work we do to solve problems.
3. We have seen that traditions of the church and the family help us to prepare for the coming of Christmas.

Take about 5 minutes for each family to recall as many of the events in the Christmas story as they can. Have bibles or copies of GOOD NEWS FOR MODERN MAN available for families to use.
List on the overhead projector the events that are suggested. Don't worry about the order in which they are listed.

Suggest that at home this next week families read both Christmas stories (Matthew and Luke) and compare the things that are alike and different.

Usually we combine the stories and make one which has the main events in it.

Show the movie by Annie Vallotton and the American Bible Society A BABY NAMED JESUS. See the Bibliography for sources of the film.

Be aware of the simple lines used to convey the story.

After the movie, make wire shapes symbolizing parts of the story. Dip in liquid plastic. Add thread to hang ornament on tree. See DECK THE HALLS for more instructions for this activity.

FIFTH SUNDAY

The purpose of this session is to explore the meaning of giving gifts.

The activity is to make a gift for someone that we do not ordinarily give gifts to.

Ideas for presentation:

Leader shows the group a gift. The leader has bought the gift for someone —
Thought about the person he was buying for —
Gift should be something the person will enjoy —
Something special —

Takes time to select just the right thing. Pleasure will be received when the person opens the gift and we see the surprise and happiness on the person's face.

Giving a gift is like sending a message that says "I care about you."

We give gifts to people in our family, our friends, and strangers who we know need our love.

A meaningful tradition at Christmas time is the giving of gifts. The greatest gift of all was the gift of Jesus Christ. Jesus taught us the value of giving — It is through giving that we find ourselves.

One man learned the lesson well — His name was Nicholas. Give a brief background of who Nicholas was:

> Bishop, Rich, Discovered that giving gifts made people unhappy if they were poor people, because they could not give gifts to Nicholas. Decided the best way to give gifts was so nobody knew who the giver was.

Show the filmstrip NICHOLAS (See Bibliography)

Have each family decide on a person to give a gift to.
Think of someone who you usually don't give gifts to, but who you know would enjoy knowing you care about them.

For those having a hard time choosing someone, suggest they consider —

persons who will be in the hospital during Christmas
    veterans hospitals
        convalescent homes
            orphanages
                juvenile homes
                    jails
                        old peoples homes
                            calling the Board of Deacons in the church for names.

Have available materials for making picture plaques. See page 45 in the chapter DECK THE HALLS for instructions on how to make plaques. Suggest some member of the family should make a card to go with gift.

Announce next Sunday's activity before persons are dismissed so that they will bring musical instruments.

SIXTH SUNDAY

The purpose of this session is to celebrate by playing and singing Christmas carols.

The leader may have decided to announce this special event to the whole congregation and invited everyone to come join the class with their instruments.

We asked the local high school band teacher to provide sheet music and music stands and to be there to lead the group. We set the"band" up in a semi-circle in the middle of the Fellowship Hall and those that were not playing instruments stood around three sides of the players to sing. The first year music students came, and the older, experienced adults — some of whom are in the city's symphony were there. Every kind of instrument was welcome from standard band instruments to homemade wash-tubs, spoons and kindergarten rhythm instruments.

This celebration has become a tradition in our church because it is so much fun.

Advent Workshops for Teachers and Parents

The following outlines of workshops were used in teacher training events. It should be noted however, that many of the activities suggested for the workshop could easily be used by the teacher in the classroom with students. This is part of the value of the workshops. The teacher can take back to the classroom practical activities from the workshop.

WORKSHOP FOR TEACHERS OF YOUNGER CHILDREN

The purpose of this workshop is two-fold. One, is to provide background on an adult level so that the teachers can identify the church year calendar, and define ADVENT. The other is to provide the opportunity for teachers to identify with young children and their concepts, enabling them to identify points of similarity and differences in the child's thinking about God and Santa.

Start with THE CHURCH YEAR exercise on page 14. Do all steps or stop at step four.
List words and phrases on the chalk board that describe ADVENT.

Show the filmstrip "LORD, COME."

> Have the class add any words or phrases that they want to the list describing Advent. Discuss any new insights they may have after seeing the filmstrip.

Ahead of time you will have put pastels and pieces of paper on the tables. Explain that you are going to play a record and show some photos. (from LORD, COME! kit) You would like the class to listen, look, feel, and react to the experience. Use the pastels to express their feelings. They may draw during the presentation or wait until after it is over.

Allow time to work, then be sure to share what they have done.

Coffee break.

Ask participants to put themselves in the place of a child 5, 6, 7 years old. Have them try to remember a Christmas when they were this age. What were some of their feelings, questions, ideas. Allow plenty of time for sharing and recalling.

Read from "CHILDREN'S LETTERS TO GOD" and "CHILDREN'S LETTERS TO SANTA CLAUS." Do not tell the participants which book you are reading from.

Ask the question: What is the child's image of God, and Santa?

Use the parallel found on page 11. Discuss the observations of the class. What happens when a child no longer believes in Santa Claus? When he stops believing in Santa Claus chances are he will begin questioning the existence of God. Do we help to bring the child to a deeper concept of God? How do we do this?

Divide the participants into small groups of 4 or 5 persons to share family and church traditions and resources that may be helpful in the classroom.

Introduce resources (see Bibliography).

WORKSHOP FOR TEACHERS OF OLDER STUDENTS #1

The objectives of the workshop are to enable participants to:

— Identify major days and seasons of the church year and describe in their own words the significant meaning of each.
— Plan a variety of teaching and celebrating experiences for their class.

STEP ONE — Small Group Research

Introduce the plan of the workshop. Describe the four research groups. Encourage everyone to select one group to work in for 30 minutes.

GROUP ONE — *Days and Seasons*

Everyone receives a sheet of paper with the name of one day or season on it.

ADVENT	LENT	MAUNDY THURSDAY
CHRISTMAS	ASH WEDNESDAY	GOOD FRIDAY
EPIPHANY	PALM SUNDAY	PENTECOST

On each sheet of paper are two questions:

1. What is the origin of the day or season?

2. What is the meaning and relevance of the day or season?

Persons use several resource books to find information to answer the questions. (Books could be: THE YEAR OF THE LORD, BIBLE DICTIONARY, THE STORY OF THE CHURCH YEAR, YOUNG READERS BOOK OF CHRISTIAN SYMBOLS)

Persons select an appropriate symbol to represent their day or season and draw this symbol on the back of their paper using crayons or felt pens.

Persons arrange themselves in chronological order of the church year to share their findings with each other.

GROUP TWO — *Biblical Names and Passages*

The focus for this group is on the concept of MESSIAH and the biblical persons who offered some insight concerning the expectation and fulfillment of the Messiah.

Each person will receive a sheet of paper with the name of one biblical person:

ISAIAH	ZECHERIAH	SIMEON
MICAH	ZEPHANIAH	MARY
JEREMIAH	JOHN THE BAPTIST	

Using a Bible, Bible Concordance, and Bible Commentary look up passages related to the words Messiah, Christ, and Anointed One, Deliverer, or other words associated with Messiah in relation to the specific biblical person.

Answer two questions:

What was this person's expectation or experience of Messiah?
In what way did Christ fulfill the expectation?

Using collage materials, create a symbol or image to express the meaning of Messiah to the particular persons.

GROUP THREE — *Key words for today*

Each person receives one or more pairs of words which express the spectrum of some of the feelings and ideas associated with Advent:

a.	Doubt and Faith	e.	Darkness and light
b.	Despair and Hope	f.	Awaiting and Encounter
c.	Suffering and Joy	g.	War and Peace
d.	Bondage and Freedom	h.	Estrangement and Love

Find one or two passages of scripture which will express some of the meaning of each pair of words.

Write a sentence or two relating these word pairs to the contemporary situation in which Advent is to be experienced this year.

Select a number of photo slides or create a montage to show the meaning of these word-pairs today.

GROUP FOUR — *Compare the two Christmas Stories*

Give each person a copy of the worksheet and a GOOD NEWS FOR MODERN MAN. Each person researches the two stories, writes down the answers to the questions according to each story. Group discusses similarities and differences. Group makes up their own Christmas Story and makes a mural showing the story they have agreed on.

Worksheet —

Matthew 1:13-2:12	QUESTIONS	Luke 2:1-20
1.	In what city was Jesus born?	1.
2.	Where was Jesus born?	2.
3.	Where did Mary and Joseph live?	3.
4.	Why did they go to Bethlehem?	4.
5.	What ruler is mentioned?	5.
6.	Is a star mentioned?	6.
7.	Are angels mentioned?	7.
8.	Who shows up in Bethlehem?	8.
9.	What do they bring?	9.
10.	What voices of authority are quoted?	10.

STEP TWO — Each small group shares their findings with the whole group.

Coffee Break

STEP THREE –- Preparation for Celebration

Participants work in small groups to do specific tasks to prepare for an Advent Celebration. Persons select group of their choice. If more than six persons choose a group it may be best to have two groups doing the same task.

1. Illustrate a song with slides.
      Have available about 150 slides and slide sorter.

      Select one song to illustrate.
      Have words of songs printed.
          O COME, O COME EMMANUEL
          IS THAT ALL THERE IS
          WHO WILL ANSWER
          7 O'CLOCK NEWS
      Select slides to illustrate as many lines as possible.

2. Write a Litany
      Write a litany on theme of Advent.
      Decide on a unison response to each line.
      Write as many lines as there is time.
      During celebration group can take turns reading the lines.

3. Poetry
      Use Cinquain or Haiku forms.
      Write poems focusing on Advent.
      Prepare to present poems in celebration by reading.

4. Biblical Passage
      Decide on what scripture to use and how to present it during celebration.
      Plan to read during celebration or any other way.

5. Select a Hymn, Carol, or Folk Song
      Using available hymn and song books and records to select a hymn to share with the group.
      Plan for group to sing or listen.
      Present it in any way group decides.

6. Interpretive Movement

   Through dance, pantomime, movement, or tableau present some interpretation of a part of the message of Advent.

7. New Symbols

   Through available materials and resources group prepares one or more new symbols to communicate the message of Advent.

After work period gather for celebration. A possible order of presentation and sharing of what the small groups have prepared follows. The order will need to be adjusted for each workshop depending on who does what.

NEW SYMBOLS
LISTEN TO OR SING HYMN OR SONG
BIBLICAL MESSAGE
INTERPRETIVE MOVEMENT
SONG WITH SLIDES
POETRY
LITANY

WORKSHOP FOR TEACHERS OF OLDER STUDENTS #2

This workshop suggests activities for nine groups of three to six persons each. The leader of the workshop may choose to use only some of these activities depending on the number of persons expected to participate. The activities suggested in this workshop and the activities suggested in the previous workshop outline can be interchanged in order to create a workshop appropriate to the group of teachers attending.

Give the participants the opportunity to choose one of the small groups. It is helpful to have a ditto sheet prepared to hand out which has listed on it the groups and their instructions.

Use the resources provided or other resources that are available to complete your assignment.
If you finish before the other groups, spend time browsing among the resources on display.
Allow one hour for the groups to complete their assignments.

Group One — Write a Script for a filmstrip

— Preview the two available filmstrips.
— Select one filmstrip for which you will write a script.
— Work together to write a script for your filmstrip.
— Prepare to share your filmstrip and script with the whole group.

Group Two — Select Slides for "Silent Night and the Seven O'Clock News."

— Listen to Simon and Garfunkel recording.
— Preview slides as you listen to recording.
— Select slides to accompany recording.
— Use slide sorter to arrange slides in sequence.
— Prepare to share slides and recording with the whole group.

Group Three — Create slides to accompany script

— Read the two available scripts from filmstrips.
— Select one script for which you will create slides.
— Use Write-On slides or black exposed 35mm to create slides.
— Prepare to share slides and script with whole group.

Group Four — Interview with Cassette Recorder

— Decide on a subject which would be related to the Advent season and interesting to discover other people's points of view.
— Phrase two or three key questions to ask of other persons.
— Practice with recorder and interview technique.
— Interview ten or more persons in the group.
— Prepare to share recording with whole group.

Group Five — Create a Game with Scripture Cards

- — Become familiar with packs of scripture cards.
- -- Brainstorm ways cards could be used.
- — Create a game involving the cards.
- — Play the game among yourselves to test it.
- — Prepare to share your game with whole group.

Group Six — See Filmstrip, "LORD, COME" and write Litany

- — See filmstrip and listen to narration.
- — Discuss several questions
    - — What do you think of the approach (art & text) of the filmstrip?
    - — What is the author's primary intention with the filmstrip?
    - — What insight have you gained about Advent?
- — Complete the statement, "Advent is . . . ."
- — Decide on a group response for the litany.
- -- Prepare to share your statements and involve the whole group in your litany.

Group Seven — Developing Individual Instruction Module

- -- Use cassette recorder with GOOD NEWS FOR MODERN MAN and Spirit Master.
- — Decide on one subject to focus upon.
- — Develop a sequence of instructions and activities to involve a student, or several students, for at least fifteen minutes.
- — Prepare cassette tape and worksheet for student to use.
- — Prepare to share your instructional module with whole group.

Group Eight — Present Church Year with Overhead Projector

- -- Use the book THE YEAR OF OUR LORD to explore meanings of the major days and seasons of the church year.
- — Decide on a way to present an overview of the church year using the overhead projector.
- — Prepare to share the results of your work with the whole group.

Group Nine — A Polaroid Camera and the GOOD NEWS FOR MODERN MAN

- — Select a parable of Jesus to be your focus.
- — Decide on a way to involve students in the exploration of the parable using a polaroid camera.
- — Use polaroid camera to demonstrate your activity.
- — Prepare to share your work with the whole group.

Provide the opportunity for each group to share with the whole group. Discuss briefly the value of these exercises in the classroom, what age groups they are appropriate for and ways they could be used. Close with prayer.

Four Sundays in Advent - A Family Liturgy *

In the Christian calendar the year begins with ADVENT. ADVENT is the period of four weeks preceding Christmas. The word "Advent" means literally "coming" and refers to the coming of Jesus as anticipated by the prophets. "Coming" also refers to Christ *has* come and Christ *will* come.

ADVENT is a time of preparation and anticipation. The meaning and joy of Christmas cannot be grasped hurriedly. The wisdom of ADVENT is that it gives us the time we need to prepare ourselves and to grow into the joy of Christmas.

ADVENT is a time for new planning, new attitudes and new inspiration for Christian families. ADVENT is one of the best times of the year — and not just for children. It is a time when families can draw closer together in their anticipation and celebration of God's gift to the world — His Son the Christ.

CELEBRATING ADVENT

Because Advent is such a meaningful time of the year there are many ways a family could celebrate Advent. One way is to make a family Advent wreath

One way is to use this chapter, to add to the suggestions in it, and to develop a family tradition of celebrating Advent during the four weeks prior to Christmas.

To accompany this chapter an Advent Wreath can be made or purchased. All that is needed is:
— a circular piece of styrofoam or other material for base.
— four candles (White or Purple) and a fifth candle if desired to be lighted on Christmas Eve as the "Christ Candle."
— Some evergreen branches or clippings.

There is much meaning in the symbolism of the Advent Wreath:
The wreath is *round,* with no beginning or end, testifying to the eternity of God's creation, of of His love and care for man.
The wreath is of *evergreen,* recalling that our faith, our hope and our love are always alive when they spring from God and His Son.

*This chapter, FOUR SUNDAYS IN ADVENT is also available in pamphlet form so that churches can purchase the pamphlet in quantity and give it to members of the congregation to use in their celebration of Advent. The pamphlet also includes suggestions for family activities and a description of the meaning of Advent. Write to Griggs Educational Service, 1731 Barcelona St., Livermore, California 94550, for information on prices for this pamphlet.

The *candles* represent the one who said, "I am the light of the world." There are four candles each representing a Sunday in Advent.

For other suggestions of ways to celebrate Advent in the home, see the chapter CELEBRATING ADVENT IN THE FAMILY.

THE FIRST WEEK IN ADVENT

Light the first candle as the family says together:

"Jesus said, 'I am the light of the world, he who follows me will not walk in darkness, but will have the light of life.'"

A child asks: *"Why do we light one candle?"*

A parent responds: *"This candle reminds us of the light of hope that the prophets had in their expectation of a Messiah who would bring peace and love to the world."*

Read what the prophets hoped for when they thought and prayed about what God would do for his people.

"The people who walked in darkness have seen a great light; those who dwelt in a land of deep darkness on them has light shined." (Isaiah 9:2)

"The Lord himself will give you a sign. Behold a young woman is with child and shall bear a son, and shall call his name Emmanuel (which means 'God with us')."
(Isaiah 7:14)

Sing or listen to recording O COME, O COME, EMMANUEL

O Come, O Come, Emmanuel, and ransom captive Israel,
That mourns in lonely exile here Until the Son of God appear.

Rejoice! Rejoice! Emmanuel shall come to thee, O Israel!

O Come, thou Wisdom from on high, Who ord'rest all things mightily;
To us the path of knowledge show, and teach us in her ways to go.

Rejoice! Rejoice! Emmanuel shall come to thee, O Israel!

PRAY —

"Dear God, our world is in darkness. We need the light of peace and love to shine in our world. Help us to prepare our lives and our homes to receive the One who said, 'I am the light of the world'. We pray in the name of Christ our Lord, Amen."

31

Light two candles as the family says together:

"Jesus said, 'I am the light of the world, he who follows me will not walk in darkness, but will have the light of life."

A child asks: *"Why do we light two candles?"*

A parent responds: *"The first candle reminds us of the light of hope of the prophets. The second candle reminds us of the dark night when Joseph and Mary found light and warmth in the stable."*

Read about the search for a place for Joseph and Mary to spend the night . . . Luke 2:1-7.

Sing   O LITTLE TOWN OF BETHLEHEM

"O little town of Bethlehem, How still we see thee lie!

Above thy deep and dreamless sleep the silent stars go by;

Yet in the dark street shineth the everlasting light;

The hopes and fears of all the years are met in thee tonight.

For Christ is born of Mary and gathered all above,

While mortals sleep, the angels keep their watch of wondering love.

O morning stars, together proclaim the holy birth;

And praises sing to God our King, and peace to men on earth!

PRAY —

"Dear God, help us to have room in our hearts and our homes for other persons who need us. We thank you for friends and strangers who have received us when we were lonely or afraid or tired. May we be ready to receive the love God offers us in Jesus. We pray in the name of Christ our Lord, Amen."

Light three candles as the family says together:

"Jesus said, 'I am the light of the world, he who follows me will not walk in darkness, but will have the light of life.'"

A child asks: *"Why do we light three candles?"*

A parent responds: *"The first candle is a reminder of the light of hope of the prophets. The second candle is a symbol of the light and warmth Joseph and Mary found in the stable. The third candle reminds us of the great light and joy which surrounded the shepherds at the announcement of Jesus' birth."*

Read the story of the Shepherd's search for the newborn Jesus. Luke 2:8-20.

Sing or listen to THE FIRST NOEL

p. 81 hymnal

"The first Noel, the angels did say,
was to certain poor shepherds in the fields as they lay;
In the fields where they lay
keeping their sheep on a cold winter's night
that was so deep.
Noel, Noel, Noel, Noel, born is the King of Israel."

WHILE SHEPHERDS WATCHED THEIR FLOCKS

"While shepherds watched their flocks by night
all seated on the ground, the angel of the Lord came down,
And glory shone around, and glory shone around."

PRAY —

"Dear God, we thank you for your gift of Jesus to the whole world. As the shepherds found Jesus in a manger, may we find Jesus in the love and joy that we share together. Help us, O God, to love one another. Help us to do our share to bring happiness, goodness and peace to the world. ..Amen."

FOURTH WEEK IN ADVENT

Light four candles as the family says together:

"Jesus said, 'I am the light of the world, he who follows me will not walk in darkness, but will have the light of life."

A child asks: *"Why do we light four candles?"*

A parent responds: *"The first candle is a reminder of the light of hope of the prophets. The second candle is a symbol of the light and warmth Joseph and Mary found in the stable. The third candle reminds us of the great light and joy which surrounded the shepherds at the announcement of Jesus' birth. The fourth candle reminds us of the ~~light of the stars in the sky which guided the Wisemen to Jesus and which keeps watch over us by night.~~* angels who announced Jesus' birth

Read the story of the birth of Jesus as Matthew wrote it.   — Matthew 1:18-2:12.

Sing or listen to WE THREE KINGS

Hymn # 83

> We three kings of Orient are; Bearing gifts we traverse afar.
> Field and fountain, moor and mountain, following yonder star.
>
> O Star of wonder, star of night, star with royal beauty bright.
> Westward leading, still proceeding, guide us to thy perfect light.

PRAY —

"O God, when we think of Christmas we think of love and lights and gifts and happy times. But, most of all, we think of Jesus, born in a manger and grown up as a loving teacher. Help us to live the way Jesus teaches us so that we may show the real meaning of Christmas.   Amen."

Light four candles and a special "Christ
Candle" if one is provided as the family
says together:

*"Jesus said, 'I am the light of the world,
he who follows me will not walk in darkness, but will have the light of life."*

Read the Christmas message from Holy
Scripture. Matthew 1:18-2:12,
Luke 2:1-20

SING —

O COME, ALL YE FAITHFUL

O come, all ye faithful, joyful and
triumphant,
Come ye, O come ye to Bethlehem!
Come and behold Him, born the King
  of angels!
O come, let us adore Him,
O come, let us adore Him,
O come, let us adore Him, Christ the Lord!

Yea, Lord, we greet Thee,
Born this happy morning,
Jesus, to Thee be glory giv'n
Word of the Father,
Now in flesh appearing,
O come, let us adore Him,
O come, let us adore Him,
O come, let us adore Him, Christ the Lord!

Hymn 89

CHRISTMAS IS . . . .

READ —

CHRISTMAS IS . . .

A DAY . . . . yesterday, today, tomorrow . . .
in the year of our Lord.

A GIFT . . . . God's gift to the world . . .
his son.

. . . Man's gift to his neighbor . . . .
acceptance and understanding.

A PARADOX . . . . Love in a world of indifference,
. . Peace in a world of war,
. . Plastic presents in a world of empty stomachs.

CELEBRATING . . . with a great feast . . . .
what about faith?

. . . with buying, wrapping, sending gifts . . .
what about THE GIFT?

. . . with songs of good cheer and Christmas Spirit . . .
what about the Spirit of Christ?

LOTS OF THINGS . . . trees, candles, lights, cards,
stockings, stars, carols, and Santa
Claus.

BUT MOSTLY CHRISTMAS IS . . .

"To you is born a savior."
"God in Christ reconciling the world to himself."
"And His name shall be called Emmanuel . . . God with us."
"The word became flesh and dwelt among us."
"God so loved the world that he gave his only Son."

Donald L. Griggs

36

JOY TO THE WORLD

SING —

"Joy to the world! The Lord is come;
Let earth receive her King;
Let every heart prepare him room,
And heaven and nature sing,
And heaven and nature sing,
And heaven, and heaven, and nature sing.

Joy to the world! The Saviour reigns;
Let men their songs employ,
While fields and floods
Rocks, hills, and plains,
Repeat the sounding joy,
Repeat the sounding joy,
Repeat, repeat the sounding joy."

PRAY —

*"O, Holy Child of Bethlehem,
Descend to us we pray;
Cast out our sin and enter in,
Be born in us today.
We hear the Christmas angels,
The great glad tidings tell,
O come to us, abide with us,
Our Lord Emmanuel.   Amen."*

OTHER PASSAGES OF SCRIPTURE

About Light: . . . . Genesis 1:1-3 (God said, "Let there be light.")
Psalm 119:97-105 ("Thy word is a lamp unto my feet.")
Isaiah 9:2-6 ("The people have seen a great light.")

About Love: . . . . Matthew 22:34-40 ("You shall love . . .")
I Corin. 13 ("The greatest of these is love.")
I John 4:7-12 ("Let us love one another.")

About Gifts and Giving: . . . . . . John 3:16 ("For God so loved the world he gave.")
Matthew 7:7-12 ("Ask and it shall be given to you.")
Mark 12:35-44 (The offering of the widow)
II Corin. 9:1-15 ("Thanks be to God for his Unspeakable gift.")

About Jesus: . . . . Matthew 28:18-20 ("Go therefore and make disciples . .")
Acts 2 (Pentecost — the birth of the church)
Ephesians 4:1-7; 11-13 (oneness and gifts)
I Peter 2:1-17 (God's own people)

About the Church: . . . . I Mark 1:1-15 ("The beginning of the gospel of Jesus Christ.")
John 1:1-4, 14 ("In the beginning was the Word.")
II Corin. 5:16-20 ("God was in Christ reconciling.")
Phillippians 2:5-11 ("Born in the likeness of men.")

NOTE:

If a family celebrates the lighting of the Advent candles every night selections from the above scriptures may be included as part of the service.

Deck the Halls

Ideas and suggestions for making Christmas decorations are very plentiful in magazines this time of year. However, we would like to add our suggestions for simple, easy to make decorations that can be made *by the family*. The materials are easy to obtain. Add to the family traditions for the season by working together to decorate your home.

SYMBOLS CONNECTED WITH ADVENT

Perhaps the most common symbol is the Advent Wreath. The wreath is *round* with no beginning or end, testifying to the eternity of God's creation, of His love and care for man. The wreath is of *evergreen* recalling that our faith, our hope and our love are always alive when they spring from God and His Son. The *candles* represent the One who said, "I am the light of the world." There are *four* candles each representing a Sunday in Advent. There is sometimes a *fifth* candle which is put in the center of the wreath and lit on Christmas eve or morning to symbolize the arrival of Christ.

The color *PURPLE* is a liturgical color which symbolizes a time of waiting. It also represents the kingly aspect of our Lord. Purple is used for both Advent and Lent.

Select a BASE:

Styrofoam ring —

Make *small* holes for candles to be fitted into. The candles will fit snugly and be firm.

Cardboard cut into a ring —

Candles are put in holders and set on the wreath, or in the circle inside the wreath.

Wood ring —

Drill holes for candles.

Select your GREENS:

Evergreens with sprigs of holly —

Remember that greens dry out quickly in a warm house.

If you choose to make an evergreen wreath be prepared to make several before Christmas.

Greens should be cut into six to eight inch lengths. With wire, attach greens to base by wrapping wire around wreath catching bunches of greens as you go. Lay greens in the same direction all the way around so that the tops of each new bunch covers the stems of the last bunch that was attached to the base.

If you have a florist clay base, just stick the greens into the base. Place base in a tray of water. The wreath may last the entire four weeks.

HANGING WREATH

Make the same as
evergreen advent
wreath using a cardboard
base. Put a loop of wire
on back to attach to door.
Tie a big red bow on bottom to
brighten it up.
Add pine cones and ornaments
for added effect.

DOOR HANGING

Materials —

Pine Boughs, Wire, Pine Cones, Wide Red Ribbon

Gather some pine boughs and
select 3 long and 6 short pieces.

Take the 6 short pieces and lay
three with stems up and three
with stems down.

Overlap and tie with wire.

Select a medium length bough
and two long boughs and
attach with wire at top.

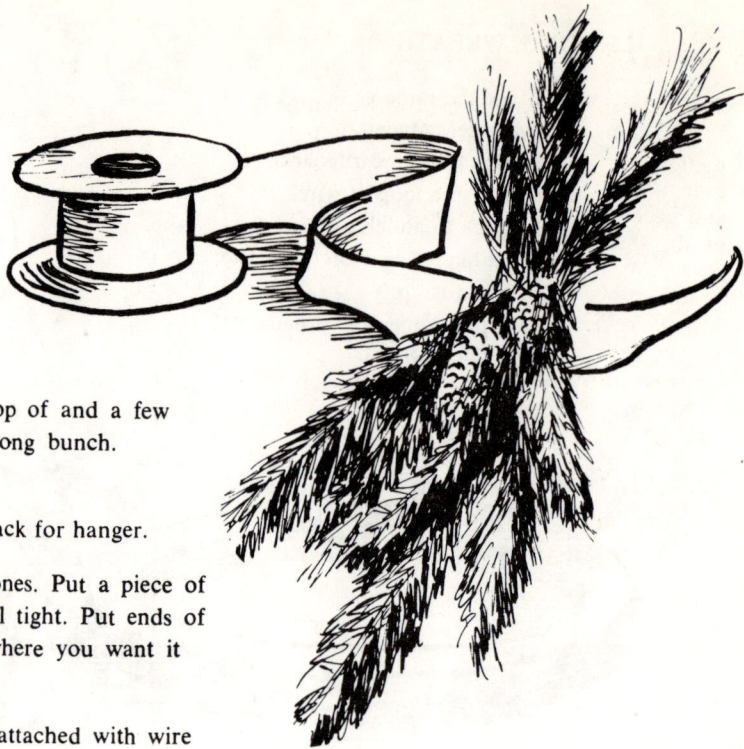

Lay small bunch at top of and a few inches below top of long bunch. Attach with wire.

Make a wire loop at back for hanger.

Decorate with pine cones. Put a piece of wire around cone, pull tight. Put ends of wire through bough where you want it and twist to hold.

A bow looks great if attached with wire at joint of boughs.

BURLAP WREATH

Materials:

One to one and a half yards of burlap in natural green or gold.

Coat hanger.

Ornaments.

1. Cut burlap into lengths 6 inches wide.

2. Ravel both sides 1¼ inches.

3. Take a wire hanger and cut next to hook.

4. Shape hanger into circle . . . .

5. Use pointed end and "sew" in stitches about one inch to 1½ inches in length down middle of burlap.

6. Gather up material as you go, letting it twist around hanger.

7. When finished twist wire back onto hook.

8. Wreath may be decorated with small ornaments, pine cones, artificial fruit, bows or whatever.

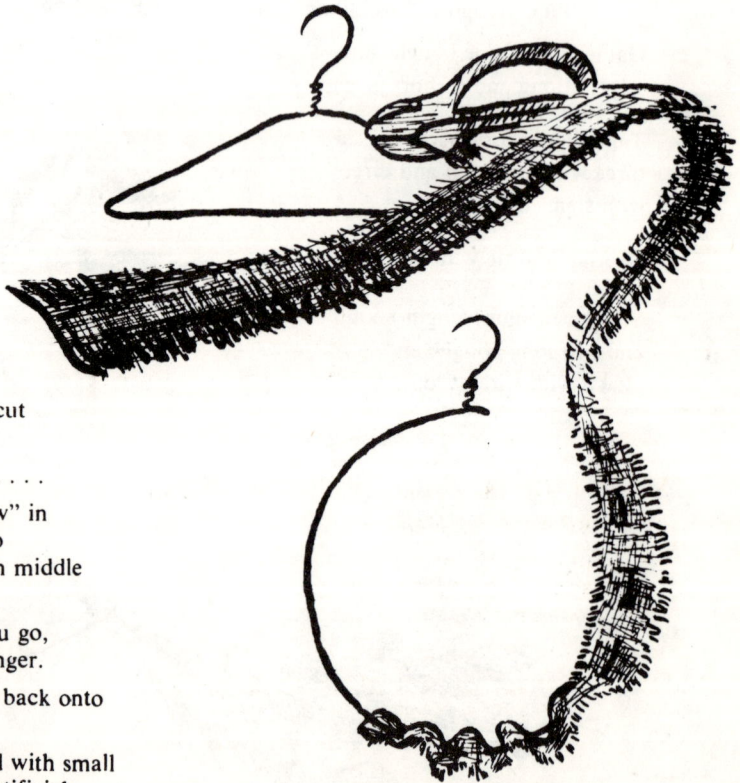

YARN WREATH

This wreath is shared by Mrs. Katherine McCrary from Charleston, West Virginia. Katherine's wreath is made from yarn pompoms attached to a styrofoam base and decorated with a big bow and figures of the three kings.

You will need:

12" styrofoam ring.
6 skeins (70 yards each) rug yarn. It is fun to use two colors, one color on the inside and one on the outside of the wreath.

Divide yarn into 10' lengths.
Make pompoms by wrapping around two cardboard circles (see diagram).

Cut around outer circle . . . tie by slipping shorter pieces of yarn between circles.
Separate circles and remove yarn.
Tie tightly and "puff out" pompom. (A great way to get rid of tension — slap the pompom on a hard surface!)
Tie pompoms on wreath as full as you want. Let the yarn cut into the styrofoam a little so it won't slip.
Add bow and other ornaments.

Circles are made from heavy cardboard.

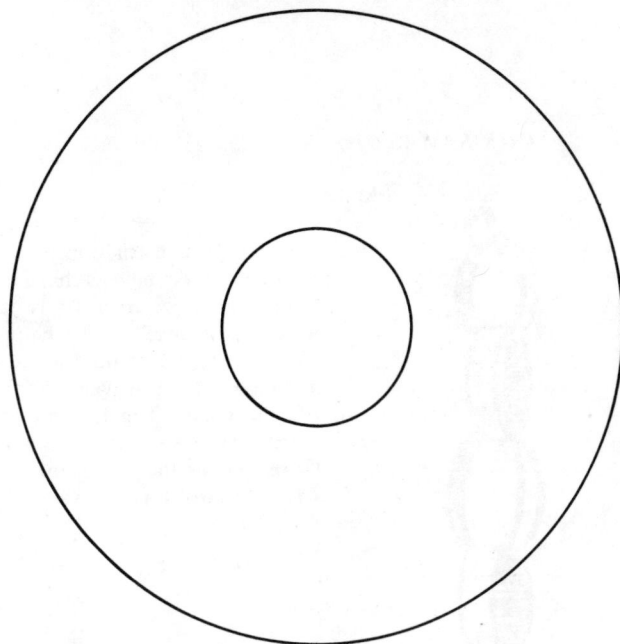

PINE CONE TREE

Materials:

> large pine cones.
> gold spray paint.
> 1 pkg. gold glitter.
> an assortment of small, tiny gold beads.
> Bottle white glue.

1. Place pine cone in box placed on its side.

2. Spray, turning cone to cover entire cone with paint.

3. Immediately after spraying while paint is still wet — sprinkle sparkles over cone.

4. When cone is dry, place gold balls in spaces between leaves. A little dab of white glue will keep them in place.

5. To finish, cone may be placed in a tray or dish and evergreens placed around the bottom.

HINTS:

> Do not let children operate spray can without supervision. Do your spraying in a well ventilated place, preferably outside.

Another possibility is to use white paint on the tips of the cone and drop silver sparkles on the paint or use colored balls.

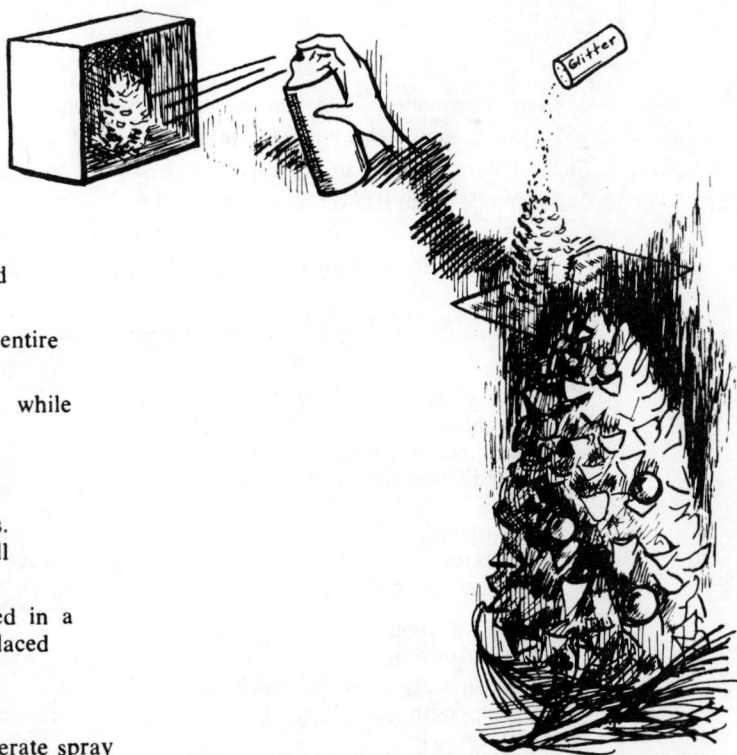

CHRISTMAS CHAIN

Materials:

One inch strips of construction paper and glue.
Small children have a hard time understanding "time."
Even with a calendar it is sometimes hard to understand how
long "two weeks" is. To help a small child begin to understand time,
let him make a chain for Advent. Put as many links as there
are days left in Advent. Each day let him take one link
off the chain. The last one may be silver or gold to represent
Christmas day. It is explained there are as many days till
Christmas as there are links in the chain.
(This is also a good way to practice counting.)

TOOTHPICK STARS

Materials:
Box of round
wooden toothpicks
1" styrofoam balls
Sparkles
Thread

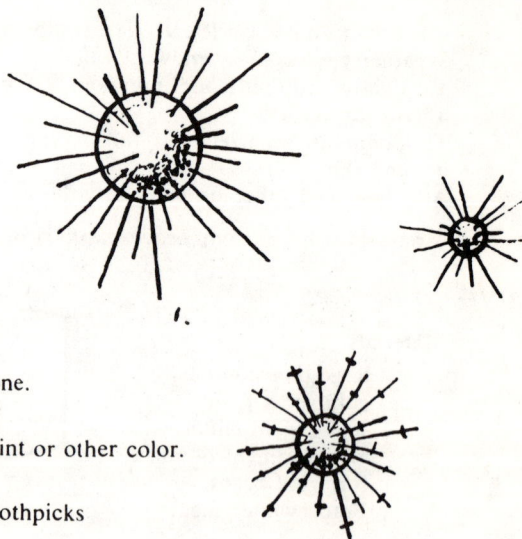

Even the smallest child can help with this one.
1. Stick toothpicks into styrofoam ball.
2. Paint ball and toothpicks with white paint or other color.
3. While paint is wet drop on sparkles.
4. Attach a black thread onto one of the toothpicks
   to hang from tree.

TIN CAN LID ORNAMENTS for older children

Materials:
Lids of cans
tin snips
small pictures from
   old Christmas cards
Glue
Nail polish
Sparkles
Thread or wire.

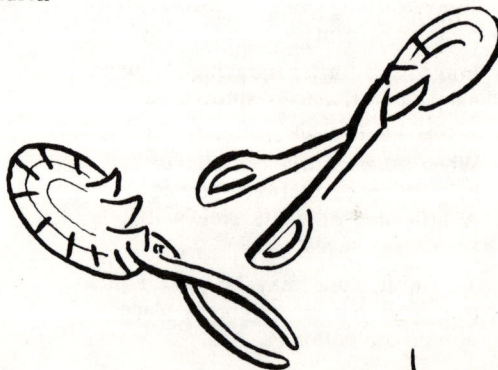

Cut into lid about 1½ to 2 inches.
Twist each section.
Glue pictures in center on each side.
With nail polish paint tips of ornaments.
Drop on Sparkles.
Attach thread or wire to hang on tree.

This technique can be used to make ornaments
out of small aluminum pie pans. The
aluminum pie pans are easier to cut and safer
for smaller children.

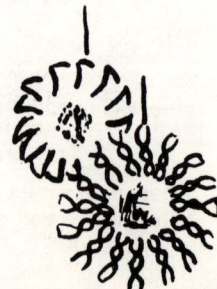

44

PLASTIC AND WIRE ORNAMENTS

Materials:

Liquid plastic and soft wire.

Bend wire into desired shape.
Dip in plastic to coat wire and fill in spaces.
Let dry.
Hang on tree
or make into mobile
or hang several on a wire across window.

PICTURE PLAQUES

Materials:

Scrap lumber
Shoe polish
Nails, chains, hammers and
    other destructive implements
Pictures
Glue
Hard floor wax
Screw-eye hanger
Pieces of felt the size of wood.

1. Select a piece of wood about 4" by 6"
   and ½" to 1 inch thick.
2. Glue a picture onto board with
   epoxy glue.
3. Let dry thoroughly (several days).
4. Hit picture and wood with hammer and
   other implements . Scar and gouge the board
   as done when antiquing wood.
5. When antiqued the way you want it use clear hard
   floor wax to cover the picture and protect
   it from the colored shoe polish.
6. Select a color of paste shoe polish that will set off
   the colors in the picture best, and rub all over wood.
7. Take soft cloth or shoe brush and polish plaque.
8. Attach decorative hanger on top of plaque.
9. Glue felt to back of plaque.

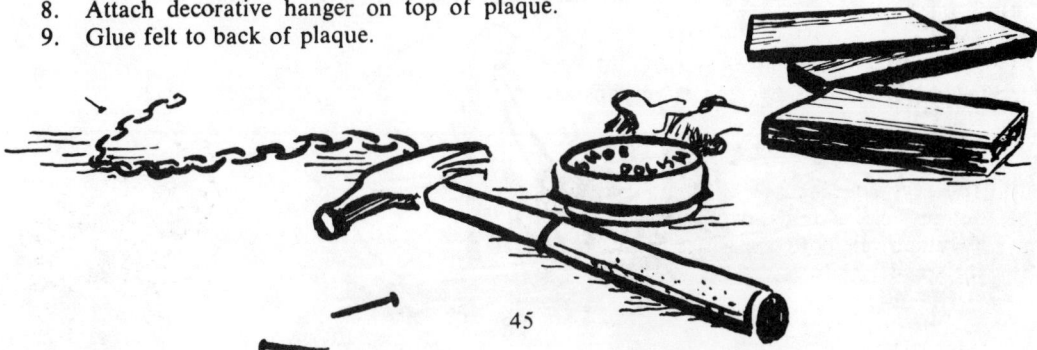

CRECHE SCENES

Materials:

Egg carton (preferably one with the long
     tall dividers that extra large eggs come in.
Sewing scraps of yardage.
Sewing trims.
White glue.
Styrofoam balls (½-inch)
Pipe cleaners.
Cotton.
Straw.
Burlap.

1. Cut off top of
egg carton, and
save it because this
will become the base
in which the scene will be placed.

Making People

2. Cut as many of the tall dividers
as you want people.
3. Put a piece of pipe cleaner in top of
divider and stick the other end into
styrofoam ball.
4. You may now dress the figure with scraps of
yardage and trims using white glue to
hold in place.
5. Pipe cleaners may be used as arms or cut part
of the egg carton for arms.

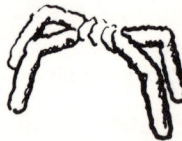

Manger

6. Cut small cup (the part the egg sits in)
and place a piece of cotton wrapped in
a strip of yardage for the baby.
7. You may want a bit of straw in the manger.

Animals

8. Sheep may be made by taking two pipe
cleaners — lay them across each other
and twist in middle.
9. Bend the ends of the pipe cleaners down.
10. Cover with cotton.

Finishing

11. Cover lid with a piece of burlap.
12. Put straw in bottom of lid.
13. Place figures of Mary, Joseph, and the Baby in the lid.
14. Place figures of shepherds and wise men around outside of carton.

46

Alternate Plan

1. Follow steps 1-3 making figures for the holy family.
2. Spray figures and carton with gold spray paint. (be sure to use spray paint that does not dissolve styrofoam.

EGG CARTON BELLS

Materials:

    Egg cartons
    Short pieces of ribbon (6")
    Paint
    Glitter
    Small Jingle Bells

1. Cut the cups from egg carton.
2. Tie a bell to end of ribbon.
3. Make a knot 2½" from bell (less if cups are small).
4. Paint egg carton cups.
5. Put on Sparkles.
6. Make small hole in top of cup and string ribbon through to knot.
7. Make loop at end of ribbon to hang on tree.

EGG ORNAMENTS

Materials:

    Shell of egg
    Plastic wrap
    Water colors
    Small pictures from
       Christmas Cards
    Thread
    Sewing scraps
    Cuticle scissors
    Wax

47

1. Punch a small hole in side of egg. (Use egg for scrambled eggs or in baking.)
2. When shell is dry, carefully cut a window in side of egg with cuticle scissors.
3. Paint inside with water colors.
4. Melt wax and pour small amount in bottom of egg.
5. Stand up small pictures in melted wax.
6. Cover window with plastic wrap cut ⅛-inch larger than window.
7. Glue in place.
8. Decorate outside of egg with rick-rack. lace, sequins, sparkles, etc.
9. Attach a thread to top of egg with glue for a hanger.

BANNERS

Materials:

   Burlap
   Felt
   Glue
   Dowel 2 inches longer than width
      of burlap
   Cord

1. Cut burlap to size of banner you want.
2. Draw design on paper.
3. Cut felt.
4. Place cut pieces on banner — do not glue until all pieces are placed correctly.
5. When satisfied with design and placement of pieces, glue on with white glue.
6. Fold over top of burlap one inch toward back of banner.
7. Sew or staple, leaving space for dowel to pass through.
8. Attach cord to dowel and hang.

A good size is 12 x18 inches. This fits in a window nicely.

A friend of ours made her banners 4 x 6 inches and sent them as Christmas cards. We put ours on the tree.

Banners may also be made in the same manner as posters or collages by using butcher paper, construction paper and collage materials.

PICTURE LIFTS

Materials:

Magazines
Heavy clear plastic
Clear contact
A table spoon
Pan of water.

1. Buy clear contact paper from hardware, variety or department store.
2. Select a picture from a "Slick paper" magazine. (covers do not work.)
3. Peel the backing off the contact paper.
4. Lay the contact smoothly over the picture. (give up if it develops a wrinkle)
5. Cut out of the magazine the picture and contact combination.
6. Place this combination of picture and contact on smooth, hard surface. Rub hard over the contact paper with the bottom of the spoon or some other smooth hard object. This process transfers the ink from the paper to the contact.
7. Place the rubbed paper and contact in a pan of warm water until you can easily separate the paper and the contact from each other. The picture (ink) should now be on the contact.
8. Dip contact with picture into the water again and with your fingers rub off the milky substance (clay base) which has remained on the sticky side of the contact.
9. Allow the new picture/contact to dry. It will be sticky.
10. Place clear plastic over sticky side to preserve picture.

Now you are ready to use your transparent picture in several ways.
a. Using small pictures, frame with construction paper and hang on tree.
b. Put picture on window — sticky side to glass after step 9.
c. Use several pictures and make a triptych by framing with light cardboard and placing a light in the middle.
d. Use several pictures framed with construction paper, some wire and thread and make a mobile.

A Child's Advent Calendar

One year when I was looking for an Advent Calendar for my children at home to use during our weekly celebration, I discovered that there were almost none that had scripture verses behind the windows. The majority had pictures of candy and popular Christmas objects and no words at all.

So, I decided to make my own calendar. I see several ways to use this calendar.

At Home —

Use a piece of felt, cloth, or paper in a purple shade which is about 24" by 18" as a base.

Cut out the shape of a Christmas tree using green construction paper or cloth that is 24" by 18" and glue to the base.

Let the children cut out the ornaments. You can make ornaments out of construction paper, old Christmas cards, or other heavy paper.

Write, type, or cut out the verses from Good News for Modern Man and glue on the inside of the ornament. Use the sheets of ornaments that are in this book and have the child color the ornaments with crayons, or decorate the outside with gummed back paper or other colored paper that has been cut to fit. Put the appropriate number of each window on the tree next to the ornament so that the windows do not have to be opened to find the right number.

When the ornaments have been glued onto the tree, let the child decorate the tree with yarn scraps, bits of rick-rack and other sewing notions, cotton, popcorn, or any other appropriate materials you have around the house.

Hang the Advent calendar in an appropriate place to be used during your Advent celebrations.

In the Classroom —

The pages of ornaments may be cut out so that you can make an electric stencil of these pages and run off copies on the church mimeograph for the various classes in the church to use. I would suggest that you use heavy weight paper in a variety of bright colors. If you use heavy white paper only, provide the opportunity for the children to decorate the ornaments before putting them on the tree, with color crayons, felt pens or other appropriate means.

We have usually made a very large tree out of green construction paper — or sometimes out of butcher paper and then colored it to put on the wall of the classroom.

This tree is usually about four feet high. Ornaments were divided up among the students to be cut out and decorated. When the student was finished with his ornaments he glued them on the tree wherever he wanted. Then he was allowed to help decorate the tree with yarn, and other collage and mosaic materials.

The windows were opened each Sunday when we lit our Advent candle at the beginning of the class time. Each Sunday we opened six new windows.

One year we had each child make his own calendar to take home and share with the rest of the family. This is a time consuming project so be sure to leave plenty of time for it if you choose to do it.

Some time should be spent helping the children understand that there is some symbolism connected with the Advent calendar.

SYMBOLS

Purple — represents the kingly aspect of our Lord.
Purple — is the liturgical color for Lent and Advent.
Green — represents life and hope.
Star — reminds us of the wise men.
Circles — remind us of the never ending love of God.
Bells — call us to worship.
Doves — represent the presence of the Holy Spirit.
Fruit — represents the giving of life God provides for us.
Packages — remind us of the greatest gift of all . . . Jesus.

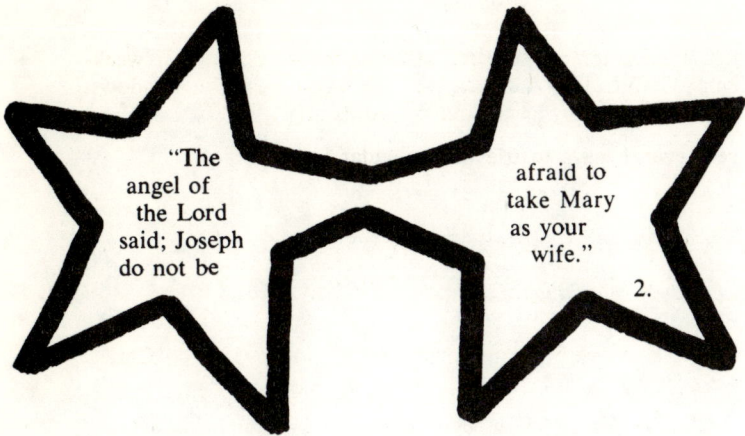

"The angel of the Lord said; Joseph do not be

afraid to take Mary as your wife."

2.

"They were terribly afraid."

10.

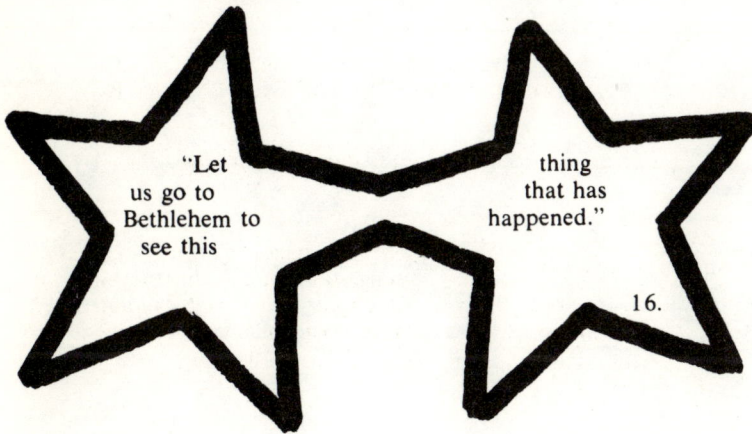

"Let us go to Bethlehem to see this

thing that has happened."

16.

"They knelt down and worshipped Him."

22.

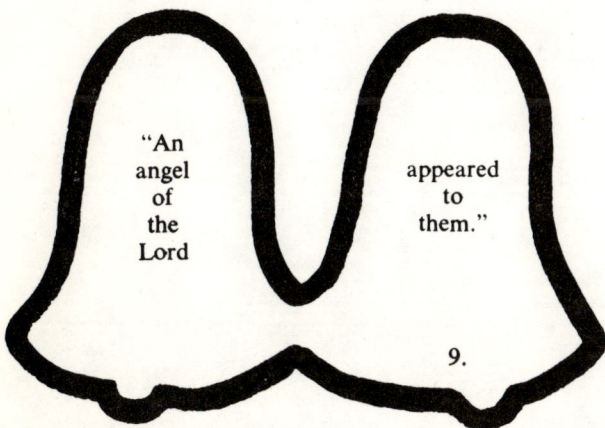

"An angel of the Lord appeared to them."

9.

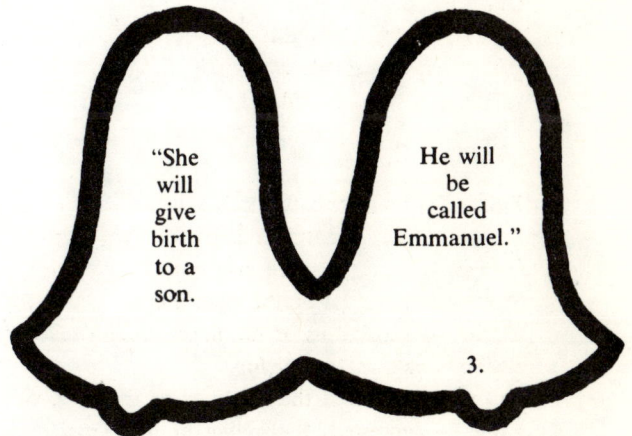

"She will give birth to a son. He will be called Emmanuel."

3.

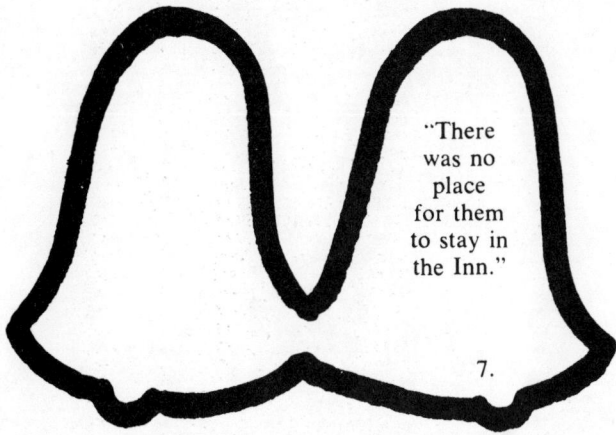

"There was no place for them to stay in the Inn."

7.

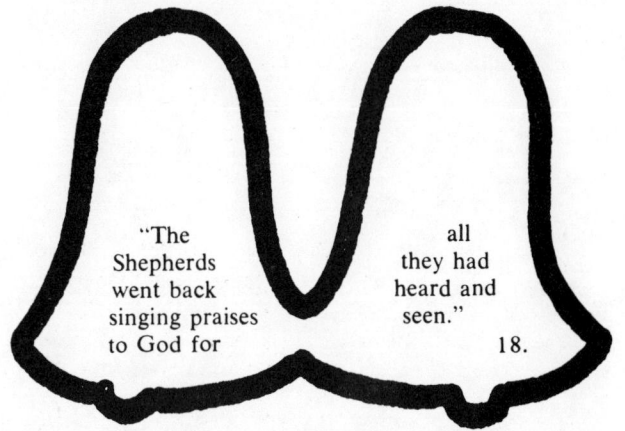

"The Shepherds went back singing praises to God for all they had heard and seen."

18.

"How happy they were when they saw the star."

20.

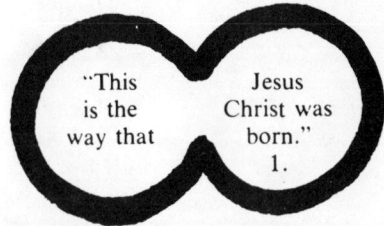

"This is the way that Jesus Christ was born."

1.

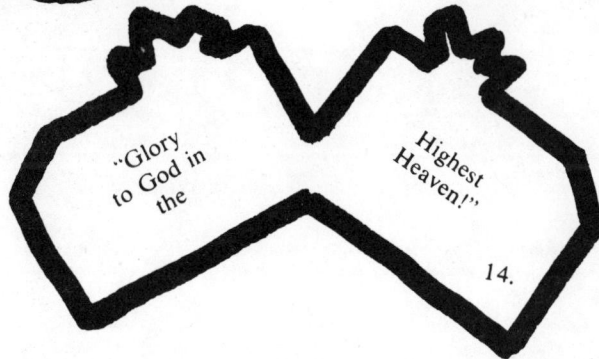

"Glory to God in the Highest Heaven!"

14.

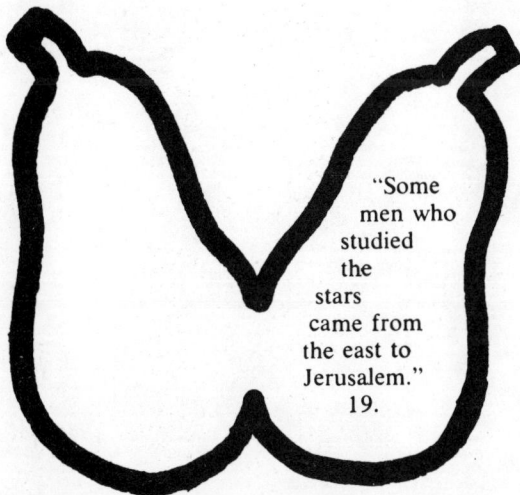

"Some men who studied the stars came from the east to Jerusalem."

19.

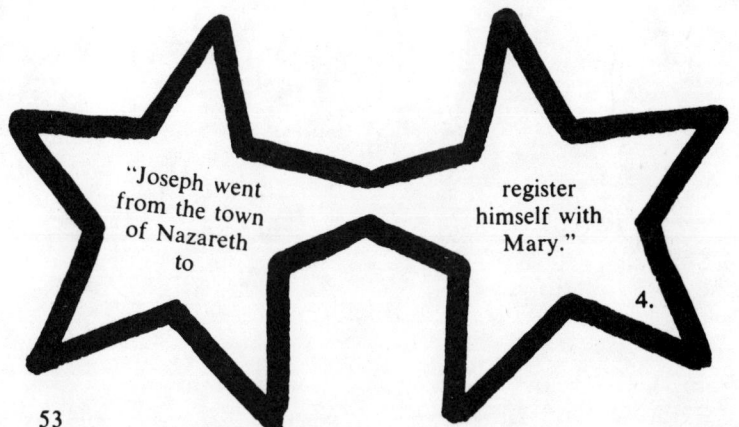

"Joseph went from the town of Nazareth to register himself with Mary."

4.

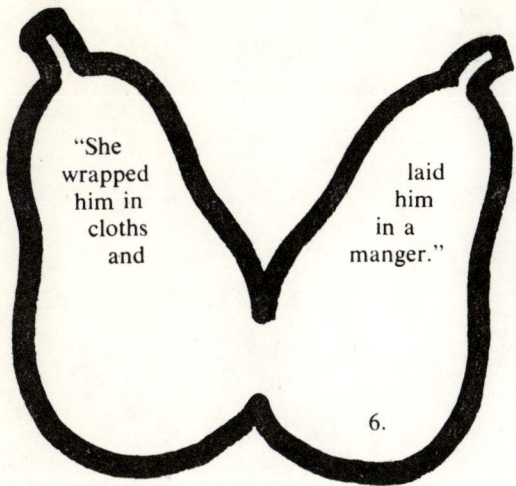

"She wrapped him in cloths and laid him in a manger."

6.

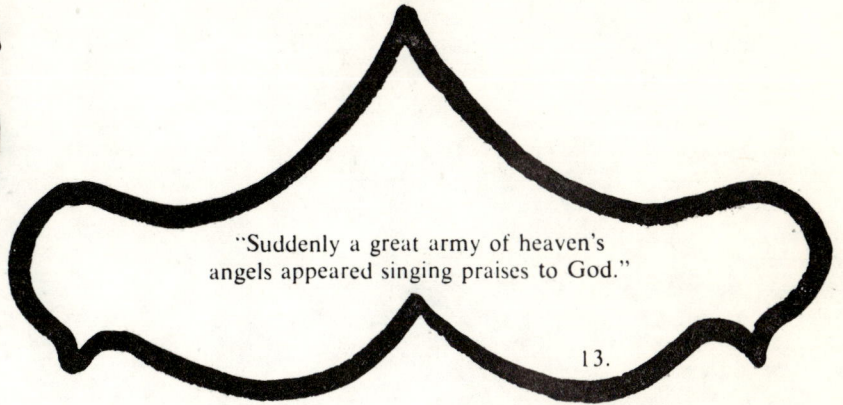

"Suddenly a great army of heaven's angels appeared singing praises to God."

13.

"There were some Shepherds in that part of the country."

8.

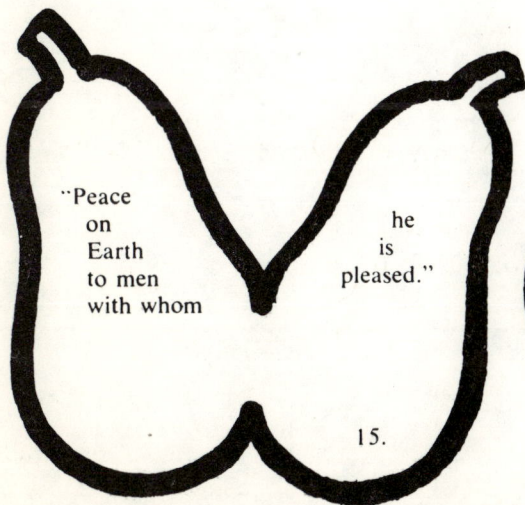

"Peace on Earth to men with whom he is pleased."

15.

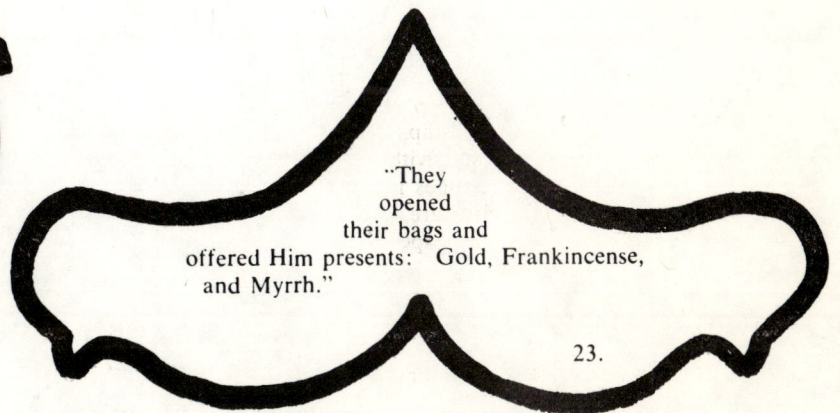

"They opened their bags and offered Him presents: Gold, Frankincense, and Myrrh."

23.

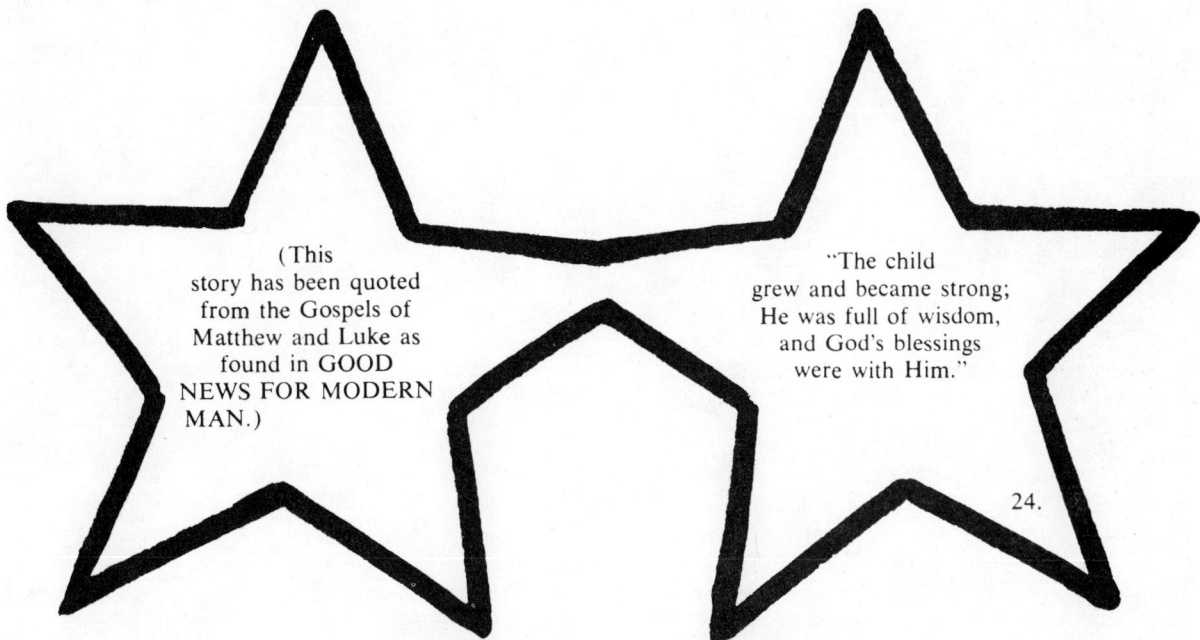

(This story has been quoted from the Gospels of Matthew and Luke as found in GOOD NEWS FOR MODERN MAN.)

"The child grew and became strong; He was full of wisdom, and God's blessings were with Him."

24.

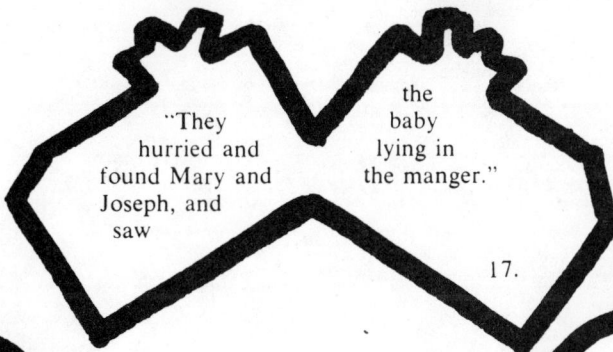

"They hurried and found Mary and Joseph, and saw

the baby lying in the manger."

17.

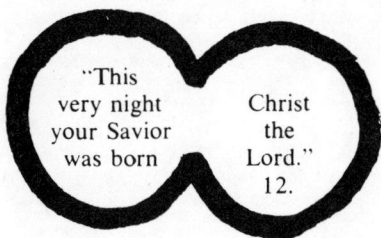

"This very night your Savior was born

Christ the Lord."

12.

"While they were in Bethlehem the time came

for her to have her baby."

5.

"But the angel said to them: Don't be afraid! For I am here with

good news for you."

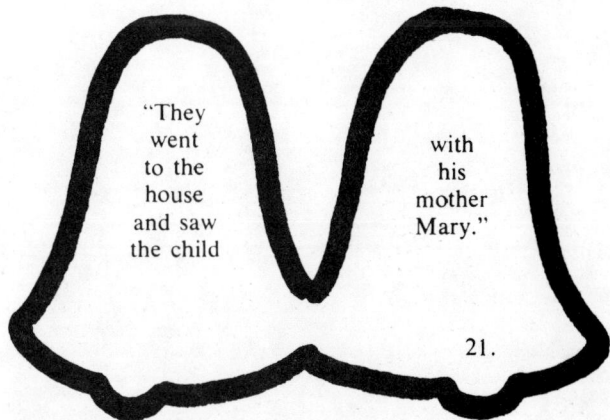

11.

"They went to the house and saw the child

with his mother Mary."

21.

57

BIBLIOGRAPHY

BOOKS

For Children —

A CERTAIN SMALL SHEPHERD, by Rebecca Caudell, Holt, Rinehart and Winston, New York N.Y. 1965.

AWAY IN A MANGER, A Story of the Nativity, by Paul Nussbaumer, Harcourt, Brace and World, Inc., N.Y. 1965.

THE BABY BORN IN A STABLE, by Janice Kramer. Concordia Publishing House, St. Louis, Missouri 1965.

BEHOLD THAT STAR — A Christmas Anthology, Edited by the Society of Brothers, Plough Publishing House, Rifton, N.Y. 1967.

BIBLE FOR YOUNG CHRISTIANS — The New Testament, by A. M. Cocagnac and Rosemary Haughton, MacMillan Co., N.Y. 1967.

CHILDREN'S LIFE OF JESUS, Hans Hoffman, Helicon, Baltimore, 1966.

CHRISTMAS BOOK, THE — (See and Hear Book and Record) by Gerry Bream, Fortress Press, Philadelphia PA 1966.

HAILSTONES AND HALIBUT BONES by Mary O'Neill, Doubleday and Company, Inc., Garden City, N.Y. 1961.

HOLY NIGHT, THE, Aurel Von Juchen, Atheneum House Inc., N.Y. 1968.

LIFE IN BIBLE TIMES by Robert Henderson and Ina Gould, Rand McNally and Co. 1967.

LITTLE DRUMMER BOY, THE, by Ezra Jack Keats, MacMillan Co., N.Y. 1968.

THANK GOD FOR CLRCLES, by Joanne Marxhausen, Augsburg Publishing House, Minneapolis, Minn. 1971.

THERE REALLY IS A SANTA CLAUS, by Glenn Crone, John Knox Press, Richmond, 1968.

THEY CAME TO SEE JESUS, by Florence Schulz, United Church Press, Boston 1962.

VERY SPECIAL BABY, THE, A Christmas Story for the Very Young, by Carol Woodard, Fortress Press, Philadelphia, PA 1968.

YOUNG READERS BOOK OF BIBLE STORIES, by Helen Doss, Abingdon Press, N.Y. 1970.

YOUNG READERS BOOK OF CHRISTIAN SYMBOLISM, by Michael Daves, Abingdon Press, N.Y. 1967.

YOUNG READERS DICTIONARY OF THE BIBLE, Abingdon Press, N.Y. 1969.

BOOKS

For the Family —

ADVENT DAY BY DAY IN THE HOME, by Liselotte Nold and Gisela Harupa, Augsburg Publishing House, Minneapolis, Minn. 1962.

CHRISTIAN FAMILY PREPARES FOR CHRISTMAS, THE, by Charles Mueller, Concordia Publishing House, St. Louis, Mo. 1965.

COME TO CHRISTMAS, Anna Laura and Edward Gebhard, Abingdon Press, N.Y. 1960.

FOUR SUNDAYS IN ADVENT, by Patricia and Donald Griggs, Griggs Educational Service, Livermore, CA 1973.

BOOKS

For Teachers —

ALL ABOUT CHRISTMAS, by Maymie R. Krythe, Harper and Brothers, New York, 1954.

CHILDRENS LETTERS TO GOD, by Eric Marshall and Stuart Hample, Essandess Special Edition, Simon & Schuster Inc., N.Y. 1967.

CHILDRENS LETTERS TO SANTA CLAUS, Bill Adler, Essandess Special Edition, Simon & Schuster Inc., 1967.

MORE CHILDRENS LETTERS TO GOD, by Eric Marshall and Stuart Hample, Essandess Special Edition, Simon and Schuster Inc., N.Y. 1967.

USE OF SYMBOLISM IN CHRISTIAN EDUCATION, THE, by Dorothy Fritz, Westminster Press, Philadelphia, PA.

WORLDS CHRISTMAS, THE, by Olive Wyon, Fortress Press, Philadelphia, PA 1964.

YEAR OF THE LORD, THE, by Theodore Kleinhans, Concordia Publishing House, St. Louis, Missouri 1967.

Picture Story Game

FEASTS/SEASONS, Christmas. By Judith Barford, George Pflaum Publishers, Inc. 1965.

RECORDS

CHRISTMAS AT MISSION SANTA BARBARA, R.C.A. Recording.
Rev. Owen de Silva O.F.M. Director, Patricia McGeehan, Narrator, Rev. Noel Maholy O.F.M. Producer. Narration is in English, Songs in Spanish. Sets scene of early California Spanish Christmas.

CHRISTMAS MUSIC IN THE HOLY LAND, Sonologue Ltd., Canton, Ohio.

COME TO BETHLEHEM, Avant Garde Records, Produced by Jack Jones, Johnny Plarson Chorus and Orchestra.

SING FOR JOY, Cathedral Films for Executive Council, Episcopal Church.

MISSA LUBA, Christmas in the Congo, Philips Label, by Les Troubodours du Roi Baudorun.

SOUNDS OF CHRISTMAS, Graded Press, Contemporary drama, music and carols related to Christmas today. Meant to be listened to by Intergenerational group and discussed.

WHAT CHILD IS THIS? World Library of Sacred Music. Narrated by Bing Crosby and Sung by the Bonventure Choir.

There are many many more records available which have Christmas music appropriate for classroom use. Because this type of record is readily availalable in the local music and record stores we have not listed them here. Rather, we have attempted to suggest some records that are somewhat unusual and that are not found in local record stores. The records listed here will probably have to be ordered through a record store, or a regional Cokesbury Book Store.

FILMSTRIPS

ADVENT, A SEASON OF HOPE, Society for Visual Education, Inc.
ADVENT LITURGY, Klise Company.
BELLS AT CHRISTMAS, Cathedral Films, Augsburg Publishing House.
CREATION AND CHRISTMAS — God's Big Promise, G. Pflaum, Publisher.
CREATION AND CHRISTMAS — The Story of Christmas, G. Pflaum.
CREATION AND CHRISTMAS — The Three Wise Men, G. Pflaum.
CHRIST AND CHRISTMAS AROUND THE WORLD, Concordia.
CHRISTMAS AGAIN, Trafco Production, Southeast Missouri State Concert Choir.
COLORS OF CHRISTMAS, Concordia, (filmstrip, slides, record, worship service guide with songs, leaders guide.)
COME ALONG WITH ME TO BETHLEHEM, Concordia.
DRAW ME A CHRISTMAS, Cathedral Films.
HE IS COMING, Augsburg Publishing House.
HOLY CHILD OF BETHLEHEM, Cathedral Films.
THE HOLY NIGHT, Weston Woods.
JESUS IS BORN, Family Filmstrips.
JOY OF GIVING A GIFT, George Pflaum.
LIGHT OF CHRISTMAS, Cathedral Films, Augsburg Publishing House.
LITTLE DRUMMER BOY, THE, Weston Woods.
LORD COME! John and Mary Harrell, Publishers.
TWELVE DAYS OF CHRISTMAS, Weston Woods.
MIRACLE OF BETHLEHEM, Lorenz Publishing Company.
NO VACANCY, Graded Press.
ST. NICHOLAS, Cathedral Films.
STORIES ABOUT CHRISTMAS CAROLS, Family Filmstrips.
STORIES ABOUT CHRISTMAS TRADITIONS, Family Filmstrips.
STORY OF HANDEL'S MESSIAH, Society for Visual Education Inc.
TELL ME ABOUT CHRISTMAS, Family Filmstrips.

16 mm FILM

A BABY NAMED JESUS, A Story Line film by Anne Vallotton. Produced by the American Bible Society.

SOURCES OF RESOURCES

AUGSBURG PUBLISHING HOUSE
426 So. Fifth Street
Minneapolis, Minn. 55415

CATHEDRAL FILMS
2921 W. Alameda, Box 1608
Burbank, California 91505

COKESBURY REGIONAL
SERVICE CENTER

CONCORDIA FILMS
3558 So. Jefferson
St. Louis, Missouri 63118

GRADED PRESS
201 Eighth Avenue So.
Nashville, Tenn. 37203

GRIGGS EDUCATIONAL SERVICE
1731 Barcelona Street
Livermore, California 94550

JOHN AND MARY HARRELL
P.O. Box 9006
Berkeley, California 94709

KLISE CO.
P.O. Box 3418
Peoria, Illinois 61414

GEORGE PFLAUM COMPANY
38 West 5th Street
Dayton, Ohio 45402

SOCIETY FOR VISUAL EDUCATION INC.
1345 Diversey Parkway
Chicago, Illinois 60614

WESTON WOODS
Weston Ct. 06880